DEVELOPMENTAL TOYS AND EQUIPMENT

DEVELOPMENTAL TOYS AND EQUIPMENT

*A Practical Guide to Selection
and Utilization*

By

ELLEN LEDERMAN, M.S., O.T.R.

CHARLES C THOMAS • PUBLISHER
Springfield • Illinois • U.S.A.

Published and Distributed Throughout the World by

CHARLES C THOMAS • PUBLISHER
2600 South First Street
Springfield, Illinois 62717

This book is protected by copyright. No part of it
may be reproduced in any manner without written
permission from the publisher.

© *1986 by* CHARLES C THOMAS • PUBLISHER

ISBN 0-398-05193-3

Library of Congress Catalog Card Number: 85-20834

With THOMAS BOOKS *careful attention is given to all details of
manufacturing and design. It is the Publisher's desire to present books that are
satisfactory as to their physical qualities and artistic possibilities and
appropriate for their particular use.* THOMAS BOOKS *will be true to those
laws of quality that assure a good name and good will.*

Printed in the United States of America
Q-R-3

Library of Congress Cataloging in Publication Data

Lederman, Ellen F.
    Developmental toys and equipment.

    Includes index.
    1. Educational   toys.   2. Play – Equipment   and
supplies.
3. Motor ability in children. 4. Child development.
I. Title.
LB1029.T6L43   1986   155.4'12   85-20834
ISBN 0-398-05193-3

155.412
L498d

To Andy...
For making it all worthwhile –

258825

PREFACE

PROFESSIONALS who work with children in any capacity recognize the importance of toys and games in promoting developmental skills and abilities. Teachers, therapists, psychologists, and other child development specialists need to carefully select toys and equipment to meet the needs of each child. To assist them with this responsibility, this book offers concrete suggestions for choosing and utilizing commercially available products.

The toys featured in the book are appealing and entertaining, but they all have additional qualities which go beyond mere entertainment. They offer an opportunity for the child to develop and practice crucial skills in the areas of gross-motor, fine-motor, sensory, sensory-motor, and visual-perceptual functioning.

There is an enormous variety of toys and games available today. While every effort has been made to present a representative sampling, it is not possible to include every product, no matter how beneficial to child development, in one volume. It is the author's hope that this book provides a starting point from which concerned adults can begin to critically analyze and creatively utilize toys as important developmental aids.

ACKNOWLEDGMENTS

THE FOLLOWING individuals and companies provided the author with photographs and information. Their assistance is deeply appreciated.

- Andrew W. Bingham, President, DLM Teaching Resources
- Candy S. Bush, Smethport Specialty Company
- Christopher Byrne, Manager, Public Relations, Ideal®, Child Guidance®, Wonder®
- Craft House Corporation
- Debbie Cullen, Senior Secretary-Marketing, Schaper Manufacturing Company
- Ellen F. Franklin, Director of Sales Promotion, Hasbro Bradley
- J.P. Grandy, Manager, Advertising/Sales Promotion, Ohio Art
- Joan Halpern, Manager of Catalogue Production and Creative Services, Childcraft
- David Eric Hancock, Marketing and Product Development Manager, Flaghouse
- Dennis J. Handwork, Director of Sales Services, Hedstrom
- HG Industries, Inc.
- Jeanne Hopkins, Public Relations, Correspondent, Milton Bradley
- Ann Hull,President, Achievement Products, Inc.
- Mary C. Janaky, Manager, Permissions, Western Publishing Company, Inc.
- Jenny Kelly, Communications Department, Kenner® Products
- Linda R. Kraus, Account Executive for Child Guidance®/Wonder®/Ideal® (CBS Toys), Schwartz Public Relations Associates, Inc.
- Louise M. Lavere, Public Relations, Fisher-Price Toys
- Laura Lawrie, Director of Marketing Services, Avalon Industries, Inc.
- Barbara Le Pore, Gerald Freeman, Inc., Public Relations for Lakeside
- Tamara Levi, Manager of Marketing Services, Flaghouse
- Yvonne K. Martin, Legal Department, Tomy
- Cynthia J. McGee, Customer Service, Reiss Toys Corporation
- Thomas G. Murdough, Jr., President, Little Tikes

- Lloyd Otterman, Chairman of the Board, Chief Executive Officer, Childcraft
- Cathy P. Pollet, Manager, Legal Administration, Tomy
- Joyce Potter, Assistant Sales Manager, Lauri
- Dean Rodenbough, Corporate Communications Manager, Binney and Smith
- Steve Schneider, Director of Research and Development, Wham-O, Inc.
- Stevens Manufacturing Company
- Barbara C. Stiles, Vice President, Marketing, Ideal School Supply Company
- Sandy Stone, Public Relations Correspondent, Milton Bradley
- Robin Storch, Marketing Services Manager, Colorforms®
- Tom Strauss, G. Pierce Toy Company
- Cathy Thorpe, Manager, Marketing and Public Relations, Mattel Toys
- William G. Todd, Vice President of Marketing, Synergistics Research
- Letitia Tompkins, Lewis Galoob Toys, Inc.
- Donna Wolf, Coordinator, Corporate Communications, Coleco

CONTENTS

DEVELOPMENTAL TOYS AND EQUIPMENT

CHAPTER 1

INTRODUCTION

TOYS ARE CRUCIAL tools for developing and improving important motor, perceptual, and sensory skills. Consequently, the toy chest of any professional who works with children can be viewed as the equivalent of the business executive's briefcase. Just as the briefcase contains important documents, papers, calculators, and other essential materials which enable the businessperson to conduct his or her business, the toys and games contained within the toy chest accomplish a similar purpose for the child development specialist. Developmental toys, games, and equipment are the means through which children learn and gain mastery of the skills and abilities which are essential prerequisites for academic and functional tasks.

Sensory, perceptual, and motor skills do not magically develop on their own. They develop and are refined through the child's active involvement in a variety of activities which demand and encourage these skills. Developmental materials need to be visually appealing and have an element of fun for them to be most effective. By eliciting the child's attention and desire to participate, important skills can be learned and practiced.

This book features toys which can be used to enhance developmental skills while providing an enjoyable, entertaining play experience. All the toys, games, and pieces of equipment are commercially available. Many of them can be found in toy stores. Others can be ordered from companies which manufacture or distribute special education materials. Some products may be discontinued after publication of this book, but the reader may be able to find or construct a similar toy to accomplish the same purpose.

Although some of the manufacturers recommend age ranges for their products, no such recommendations are made in this book. Chronological age can be viewed as relatively unimportant. Developmental age has much more significance. Professionals need to base their selection of toys on each child's strengths and weaknesses, rather than on the number of birthdays that the child has celebrated.

Similarly, the book does not address specific diagnostic categories or handicaps. Children with such diverse diagnoses as mental retardation, learning disabilities, developmental delays, physical handicaps, or emotional disturbances often have not developed certain motor, perceptual, and sensory skills. The toys in this book develop and enhance these skills which are essential for all children, regardless of their diagnostic labels.

Many toys can serve more than one developmental function. Some toys have several features, each one of which develops a different skill. A toy which develops a specific fine-motor skill may also develop a perceptual skill or a sensory-motor ability. For the purposes of organization, however, each toy, game, or piece of developmental equipment has been classified as predominantly facilitating one particular skill and placed in the category which the skill falls under...i.e. fine-motor, sensory, sensory-motor, and visual-perceptual. Other developmental skills enhanced by the toys are also noted, even if they fall under a different category than the predominant skill. To further expedite the reader's appreciation of the vast number of commercially available toys with developmental aspects, Appendix A provides a complete listing of every toy which contributes to the development of each individual skill.

Ideally, a variety of toys should be utilized to help a child gain proficiency in a skill. Aside from the obvious advantage of better maintaining the child's interest, this practice also ensures that the skills which develop won't be merely splinter skills. A child may gain competence by constantly using a toy to the exclusion of all others, but this competency might not generalize to another toy or activity. For instance, a child might achieve some proficiency with a toy or game which promotes pincer grasp or eye-hand coordination if he or she plays with that specific toy all the time, but the pincer grasp or eye-hand coordination is of limited value if it cannot be transferred to other toys. To avoid developing isolated, non-functional splinter skills, a wide variety of toys should be used.

CHAPTER 2

FINE-MOTOR DEVELOPMENT

MOST DEVELOPMENTAL and functional activities demand a certain amount of fine-motor skill. Mastery of fine-motor milestones and abilities is essential for participation in self-care, academic, and recreational activities.

Manipulative skill consists of many essential components. Reaching, although using the larger muscles of the shoulder and elbow rather than the small muscles in the hand, can be considered the preliminary step, since it enables the child to make the initial contact with an object and bring it to an optimal location for manipulation. Accurate reaching requires an integration of motor output with visual input.

The forearm position affects manipulative abilities. Certain activities require that the forearm be rotated to the "palms up" or supinated position, whereas others need to be accomplished in the "palms down" or pronated position. Still other activities are most functionally performed in a neutral forearm position, midway between pronation and supination.

Wrist position is equally important. In addition to the side to side movements of radial deviation (to the thumb side) or ulnar deviation (to the little finger side), the wrist is also capable of upward (extension) and downward (flexion) motions. Slight extension of the wrist facilitates grasping, whereas wrist flexion enables release of the objects.

Palmar/whole hand/total grasp allows the infant to hold objects, but this grasping pattern needs to be modified for the child to engage in more sophisticated manipulation. The ability to extend and probe with the index finger is necessary for the development of an inferior pincer grasp. Combined with the isolated index finger function is thumb movement to the lateral side of the index finger to enable an object to be grasped between the thumb and index finger. Continued development leads to a superior pincer grasp in which the thumb is rotated to contact the palmar surface of the last joint of the index finger. Manipulative prehension can then develop, along with finger differentiation.

Adequate muscle tone and strength enable functional manipulation. The muscle tone in the hands must be sufficiently high for the joints to maintain their stability and position in grasping, but not to the point where it is so excessively high that movement (such as releasing an object) is impeded. The amount of muscle strength needed varies according to the activity and object to be manipulated.

Fine-motor dexterity, a blending of speed and accuracy, becomes possible when the child has achieved mature prehensile development and adequate muscle strength/tone. For many complex activities, however, manipulative skill needs to be combined with other developmental elements such as visual-motor integration, bilateral coordination, motor planning, and sensory awareness.

Children can experience a delay or dysfunction in any of the components which comprise fine-motor skills. Reaching can be made difficult by spasticity or hypertonus, orthopedic abnormalities which impede joint range of motion, muscle weakness, and impaired eye-hand coordination.

The ability to position the forearm and wrist as required by the activity (i.e. forearm supination or wrist extension) may be lacking in some children; the reasons may range from muscle weakness or imbalance to developmental immaturity.

Opposition of the thumb and forefinger in a pincer grasp rather than a total hand grasp is a developmental skill which many children have trouble achieving. Even though most of them have no neuromuscular or skeletal problems which physically prevent them from using mature prehensile patterns, they frequently revert back to more primitive patterns which interfere with the attainment of fine-motor dexterity.

Low muscle tone or strength may be a result of a specific neurological disorder or may simply be traced to a lack of opportunities and experiences which develop tone and strength.

The toys and games in this chapter can be utilized to enhance fine-motor development in one or more of the following areas:

- arm and hand strength
- elbow extension
- extension of index finger
- fine-motor dexterity
- forearm pronation and supination
- grasp and release
- grasp for writing instruments
- isolated finger function
- lateral pinch
- pincer grasp
- reach
- shoulder mobility/range of motion
- use of scissors
- wrist extension
- wrist rotation

AIR JAMMER® BUG SCRAMMER

Available from:

Tomy Corporation
901 East 233 Street
P.O. Box 6252
Carson, California 90749

Available at many major toy stores

Description:

The car roars off when the engine is pumped up with air.

Developmental value:

- Pumping up the cars promotes and strengthens wrist extension.

Photo courtesy of
Tomy Corp.

AIR-MAZING GAMES™

Available from:

Tomy Corporation
901 East 233 Street
P.O. Box 6252
Carson, California 90749

Available at many major toy stores

Description:

An air-play game in which pressing the bubble activates balls through a maze.

Developmental value:

- Pressing down on the bubble to propel the balls can strengthen finger muscles.
- Visually following the movement of the balls promotes visual tracking ability.
- Pressing on the bubble to propel the balls in certain crucial places around the maze improves eye-hand coordination.

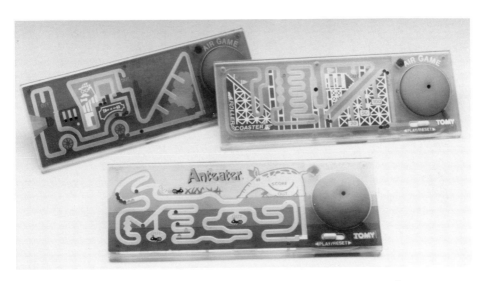

Photo courtesy of
Tomy Corp.

ANTS IN THE PANTS®

Available from:

Schaper® Manufacturing Company
P.O. Box 1426
Minneapolis, Minnesota 55440
Available at many major toy stores

Description:

One to four players try to make their ants jump into the pants by pressing a finger down on the tail of the ant and then releasing it. The object of the game is to be the first player to get all the ants into the pants.

Developmental value:

- Pressing down on the tail of an ant promotes isolated finger function, particularly of the extended index finger.
- Aiming the ants into the pants improves eye-hand coordination.

Photo courtesy of
Schaper® Mfg. Co.

AQUA ACTION™ GAMES

Available from:

Tomy Corporation
901 East 233 Street
P.O. Box 6252
Carson, California 90749

Available at many major toy stores

Description:

Pocket sized self-contained water games in which pressing the button propels tiny balls or rings towards a target.

Developmental value:

- Pressing the button develops the ability to isolate and use the thumb or index finger.
- Visually following the movement of the balls or rings promotes visual tracking ability.

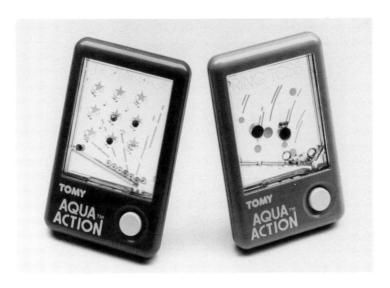

Photo courtesy of
Tomy Corp.

BED BUGS™

Available from:

Milton Bradley Company
443 Shaker Road
East Longmeadow, Massachusetts 01028-5247

Available at many major toy stores

Description:

Two to four players try to grab as many jumping bugs as possible
from the shaking motorized bed, using giant tweezer-like tongs. Each
turn only bugs of a certain color may be captured. The player with the
most bugs when the bed is empty is the winner.

Developmental value:

- Using the tongs requires and utilizes a pincer grasp.
- Grabbing the bugs as quickly as possible from the shaking bed improves eye-hand coordination and fine-motor dexterity.
- Grabbing the correct color of bugs promotes visual figure-ground discrimination and color perception.

Photo courtesy of
Milton Bradley Co.

BIG MOUTH SINGERS®

Available from:

Child Guidance®
CBS Toys, A Division of CBS Inc.
41 Madison Avenue
New York, New York 10010
Available at many major toy stores

Description:

When the keys are depressed, eight humorous characters sing out the notes.

Developmental value:

- Pressing a key develops isolated finger function.
- Pressing the appropriate key improves eye-hand coordination.
- Playing one of the color-coded songs in the songbook enhances color matching abilities.
- Hearing and playing the different musical notes can improve auditory discrimination and sound sequencing.

Photo courtesy of
Schwartz Public Relations
Associates, Inc. for
Child Guidance®/CBS Toys

BIG PEGBOARD AND STACKABLE PEGS

Available from:

Ideal School Supply Company
11000 South Lavergne Avenue
Oak Lawn, Illinois 60453

Available through the Ideal catalog

Description:

A pegboard with plastic pegs which can be stacked.

Developmental value:

- Picking up and holding the pegs develops pincer grasp.
- Placing the pegs into the holes or stacking them improves eye-hand coordination.

Photo courtesy of
Ideal School Supply Co.

Blowouts™ POWER PUMP'N CARS

Available from:

Tomy Corporation
901 East 233 Street
P.O. Box 6252
Carson, California 90749

Available at many major toy stores

Description:

Cars with an air power "gas-pump" that revs them up to zoom away.

Developmental value:

• Pumping up the cars promotes and strengthens wrist extension.

Photo courtesy of
Tomy Corp.

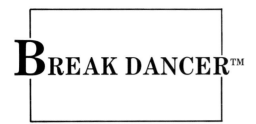BREAK DANCER™

Available from:

Tomy Corporation
901 East 233 Street
P.O. Box 6252
Carson, California 90749

Available at many major toy stores

Description:

When the long black stick is inserted into the Break Dancer's body and pulled out quickly, the dancer spins on his feet, head, or extended arm.

Developmental value:

- Holding the stick while inserting it into the body and then pulling it out encourages a lateral pinch.
- Inserting the stick into the body promotes eye-hand coordination.

Photo courtesy of
Tomy Corp.

Bron™

Available from:

Lewis Galoob Toys, Inc.
500 Forbes Boulevard
South San Francisco, California 94080

Available at many major toy stores

Description:

By using Bron's™ Power Pump to either pressurize or de-pressurize the robot upon command, he'll lift 25 times his own weight, make a car collapse, or shoot Power Spheres!

Developmental value:

- Using the pump can improve arm and hand strength, while encouraging wrist extension.

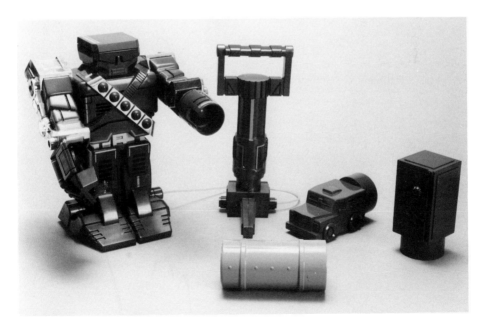

Photo courtesy of
Lewis Galoob Toys

CHINESE CHECKERS

Available from:

Steven Manufacturing Company
224 East 4th Street
Hermann, Missouri 65041-0275

Available at many major toy stores

Description:

A variation on the game of checkers, played with marbles.

Developmental value:

- Picking up each marble provides an opportunity to practice pincer grasp and release.
- Placing the marbles into the holes improves eye-hand coordination.

Photo courtesy of
Steven Mfg. Co.

CRAYOLA® YARN PICTURES

Available from:

Binney and Smith
1100 Church Lane
P.O. Box 431
Easton, Pennsylvania 18042

Available at many major toy stores

Description:

A yarn craft kit. Colored yarn is tucked into the color-coded board to make attractive pictures.

Developmental value:

- Using the tucking tool develops fine-motor dexterity and eye-hand coordination.

Pictured: Tip Toe Teddie
Photo courtesy of
Binney and Smith

CREATIVE RAILWAY

Available from:

The Little Tikes® Company
2180 Barlow Road
Hudson, Ohio 44236

Available at many major toy stores

Description:

Track pieces which can be linked together to form a variety of configurations.

Developmental value:

- Pushing the train around the track develops the ability to reach, sometimes across the midline.
- Pushing the train around the track in various configurations develops motor planning and eye-hand coordination.

Photo courtesy of
the Little Tikes Co.

CURIOUS CRITTERS™

Available from:

Tomy Corporation
901 East 233 Street
P.O. Box 6252
Carson, California 90749

Available at many major toy stores

Description:

After the animals are wound up, the remote control magnetic wand can be used to activate them to walk or wag their tails. One side of the wand attracts them, while the other causes them to turn away.

Developmental value:

- Winding up the animals develops pincer grasp.
- Flipping the wand from one side to the other promotes forearm pronation and supination.

Photo courtesy of
Tomy Corp.

DAPPER DAN

Available from:

Smethport Specialty Company
One Magnetic Avenue
Smethport, Pennsylvania 16749

Available at many major toy stores

Description:

A magnetic pencil moves iron powder around the face to create different hair styles, eyebrows, mustaches, and beards.

Developmental value:

- Holding the magnetic pencil improves the ability to hold onto a writing instrument.
- Moving the powder to create a specific design develops eye-hand coordination.

Photo courtesy of
Smethport Specialty Co.

DELUXE AGGRAVATION®

Available from:

Lakeside
495 Post Road East
Westport, Connecticut 06880

Available at many major toy stores

Description:

A board game for two to six players in which marbles are moved from the starting base to the "home" area. A die is tossed to determine the play. When one marble lands on another, the first marble is "aggravated" back to start.

Developmental value:

- Picking up the marbles requires and refines pincer grasp.
- Placing the marbles into the holes improves eye-hand coordination.

Photo courtesy of
Gerald Freeman, Inc.
Public Relations for
Lakeside

DOGGONE DOG®

Available from:

Tomy Corporation
901 East 233 Street
P.O. Box 6252
Carson, California 90749

Available at many major toy stores

Description:

By pushing down his hat, the dog's ears drop, eyes open, nose and tongue pop out...then he waves his arms and scoots away.

Developmental value:

- Pushing down the hat develops wrist extension.
- Pressing down on the hat improves hand strength.

Photo courtesy of
Tomy Corp.

DON'T SPILL THE BEANS®

Available from:

Schaper® Manufacturing Company
P.O. Box 1426
Minneapolis, Minnesota 55440

Available at many major toy stores

Description:

Two to four players take turns dropping one bean at a time onto the pot, carefully trying not to tip the pot. The winner is the first player to get rid of all his or her beans.

Developmental value:

- Picking up the beans develops and improves pincer grasp.
- Dropping the beans onto a place on the pot where it will balance and not tip the pot over enhances eye-hand coordination.

Photo courtesy of
Schaper® Mfg. Co.

DOODLE BALLS

Available from:

Smethport Specialty Company
One Magnetic Avenue
Smethport, Pennsylvania 16749

Available at many major toy stores

Description:

The magnetic pencil moves the enclosed balls to various positions on the grid.

Developmental value:

- Holding the magnetic pencil improves the ability to hold onto a writing instrument.
- Pressing down on the plastic covering to contact with the ball and move it to the desired location improves grasp strength.
- Moving the balls to specific holes to form a design enhances eye-hand coordination and visual space and form perception.

Photo courtesy of
Smethport Specialty Co.

DRAGON® CHINESE CHECKERS

Available from:

Milton Bradley Company
443 Shaker Road
East Longmeadow, Massachusetts 01028-5247

Available at many major toy stores

Description:

Pegs, rather than marbles, are utilized in this classic game.

Developmental value:

- Picking up each peg provides an opportunity to practice pincer grasp and release.
- Placing the pegs into the holes improves eye-hand coordination.

Photo courtesy of
Milton Bradley Co.

ELECTRONIC MUSICAL PHONE™

Available from:

Playskool®, Inc.
A Hasbro Bradley Company
1027 Newport Avenue
Pawtucket, Rhode Island 02862

Available at many major toy stores

Description:

A musical phone with a twelve note keyboard that plays hundreds of songs.

Developmental value:

- Pressing each key requires and develops the use of an extended index finger.
- Pressing each key strengthens the finger muscles.
- Playing a color or number-coded song develops color and number matching skills.
- Hitting the desired keys improves eye-hand coordination.
- Hearing and playing the different musical notes can improve auditory discrimination and sound sequencing.

Photo courtesy of
Playskool®, Inc.

FRISBEE® DISC

Available from:

Wham-O®, Inc.
835 East El Monte Street
P.O. Box 4
San Gabriel, California 91778-0004

Available at many major toy stores

Description:

A plastic disc which is tossed in the air.

Developmental value:

- Tossing the frisbee requires and develops wrist extension and rotation, as well as elbow extension.
- Catching a frisbee promotes eye-hand coordination.

Photo courtesy of
Wham-O®

GHOSTS!®

Available from:

Milton Bradley Company
443 Shaker Road
East Longmeadow, Massachusetts 01028-5247

Available at many major toy stores

Description:

A glow-in-the-dark game in which two players each have four "good" ghosts and four "bad" ghosts. The identity of each ghost is concealed from the opponent. By moving one space at a time, players try to sneak their "good" ghosts out a door on the opponent's side or to capture the opponent's four "good" ghosts.

Developmental value:

- Picking up the ghosts promotes pincer grasp.

Photo courtesy of
Milton Bradley Co.

GO GO GUYS™

Available from:

Tomy Corporation
901 East 233 Street
P.O. Box 6252
Carson, California 90749

Available at many major toy stores

Description:

The fireman or pilot move on their own or in one of their vehicles when their heads are pushed down.

Developmental value:

- Pushing down the heads promotes and strengthens wrist extension.

Photo courtesy of
Tomy Corp.

HI-HO! CHERRY-O® GAME

Available from:

Western Publishing Company, Inc.
1220 Mound Avenue
Racine, Wisconsin 53404

Available at many major toy stores

Description:

A counting game which incorporates "picking" plastic cherries from the gameboard.

Developmental value:

- Picking up the cherries provides an opportunity to practice pincer grasp and release.

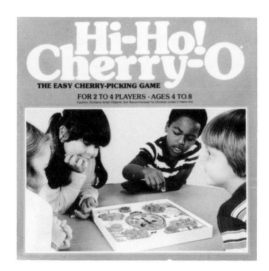

Photo courtesy of
Western Publishing Co.

 Hilarious hats™

Available from:

Tomy Corporation
901 East 233 Street
P.O. Box 6252
Carson, California 90749

Available at many major toy stores

Description:

Hats which spin around and then open up to reveal their faces when wound up.

Developmental value:

- Winding up the toys requires and develops pincer grasp.

Photo courtesy of
Tomy Corp.

 Hᴵ-Q® GAME

Available from:

Ideal®
CBS Toys, A Division of CBS Inc.
1107 Broadway
New York, New York 10010

Available at many major toy stores

Description:

One player tries to jump the pegs until there's just one left.

Developmental value:

- Picking up each peg requires and develops pincer grasp.
- Placing the pegs into the holes improves eye-hand coordination.
- Planning the order of pegs to jump over enhances strategic thinking skills.

Photo courtesy of
Schwartz Public Relations
Associates, Inc. for
Ideal®/CBS Toys

HUNGRY HUNGRY HIPPOS®

Available from:

Milton Bradley Company
443 Shaker Road
East Longmeadow, Massachusetts 01028-5247

Available at many major toy stores

Description:

Two to four players push a lever to make their hippo stick his long neck out and swallow each marble as it is shot onto the tray. The winner is the player whose hippo swallows the most marbles.

Developmental value:

- Pressing the lever to make the hippo reach out develops the ability to isolate and use an extended index finger.
- Pressing down on the lever at the appropriate time to cause the hippo to swallow the marble improves eye-hand coordination.
- Watching the movement of the marble as it rolls around the tray promotes visual tracking skills.
- Picking up the marbles to set up a new game develops pincer grasp.

Photo courtesy of
Milton Bradley Co.

INCREDIBLE THRASHER™

Available from:

Lewis Galoob Toys, Inc.
500 Forbes Boulevard
South San Francisco, California 94080

Available at many major toy stores

Description:

When the grip handle of the action vehicle is squeezed, a soft spiked ball whirls around and around to ward off the enemy.

Developmental value:

• Squeezing the handle can improve grasp strength.

Photo courtesy of
Lewis Galoob Toys

JUMBO® TIDDLEDY WINKS

Available from:

Milton Bradley Company
443 Shaker Road
East Longmeadow, Massachusetts 01028-5247

Available at many major toy stores

Description:

By pressing down on the large wink with the giant wink, two to four players attempt to get the highest score by landing the wink into the cup or on a high number on the scoring board.

Developmental value:

- Holding and pressing down with the giant wink develops and strengthens pincer grasping ability.
- Aiming the wink into the cup improves eye-hand coordination.

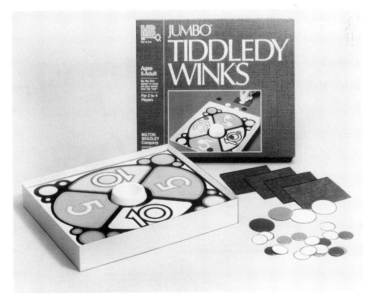

Photo courtesy of
Milton Bradley Co.

#

Available from:

Ideal®
CBS Toys, A Division of CBS Inc.
1107 Broadway
New York, New York 10010

Available at many major toy stores

Description:

Marbles are suspended on a nest of plastic sticks. Players remove the sticks one by one until someone pulls out a crucial stick and marbles fall down. The winner is the player with the fewest marbles.

Developmental value:

- Pulling out a single stick develops and improves pincer grasp.
- Picking up the marbles that have dropped develops and improves pincer grasp.

Photo courtesy of
Schwartz Public
Relations Associates,
Inc. for Ideal®/CBS Toys

LARGE PEGBOARD AND PEGS SET

Available from:

Lauri, Inc.
Phillips-Avon, Maine 04966

Available through many special education catalogs

Description:

A crepe foam rubber pegboard with enameled hardwood pegs.

Developmental value:

- Inserting or removing the pegs provides a strengthening exercise for the hands, as the friction-fit holes offer a slight resistance.
- Grasping the pegs when picking them up, inserting them, or removing them encourages a refined pincer grasp.
- Placing the pegs into the holes enhances eye-hand coordination.
- Arranging the pegs according to a specific pattern improves visual-spatial perception.

Photo courtesy of
Lauri, Inc.

LEVERAGE™

Available from:

Milton Bradley Company
443 Shaker Road
East Longmeadow, Massachusetts 01028-5247

Available at many major toy stores

Description:

Two players try to advance their pawns of different sizes and weights to their opponent's safety zone without losing their scoring pegs. When the uniquely suspended gameboard tips towards a player, he or she must give up one or more pegs to balance the board.

Developmental value:

- Picking up and holding the pegs enhances pincer grasp.
- Inserting the pegs into the holes improves eye-hand coordination.

©1982 by Jack B. Slimp, Jr.

Photo courtesy of
Milton Bradley Co.

LIGHT AND LEARN™

Available from:

Milton Bradley Company
443 Shaker Road
East Longmeadow, Massachusetts 01028-5247

Available at many major toy stores

Description:

Using one of the quiz cards, one or more players select the appropriate answers by inserting the electric probe into the hole in the answer box. Correct answers cause the probe to light up.

Developmental value:

- Holding the probe develops the ability to hold a writing utensil.
- Inserting the probe into the hole in the answer box improves eye-hand coordination.

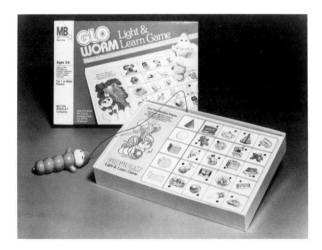

Pictured: Gloworm™ Light and Learn Game© 1985 Hasbro Bradley, Inc.

Photo courtesy of
    Milton Bradley Co.

LITE-BRITE®

Available from:

Hasbro Bradley Industries, Inc.
1027 Newport Avenue
P.O. Box 1059
Pawtucket, Rhode Island 02862-1059

Available at many major toy stores

Description:

After pictures are designed with the colored pegs, the console can be
turned on to light up the pictures. Color coded pictures can be placed
on top of the pegboard.

Developmental value:

- Picking up the pegs improves pincer grasp and release.
- Inserting the pegs onto the color coded pictures enhances eye-hand
  coordination.

Photo courtesy of
Hasbro Bradley, Inc.

LITTLE TOOTER TRUMPET®

Available from:

Tomy Corporation
901 East 233 Street
P.O. Box 6252
Carson, California 90749

Available at many major toy stores

Description:

Plays "Mary Had A Little Lamb" as the buttons are pushed.

Developmental value:

- Pressing down on the buttons promotes isolated finger function.

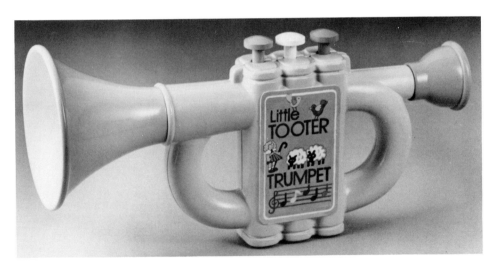

Photo courtesy of
Tomy Corp.

Magic "8 Ball"®

Available from:

Ideal®
CBS Toys, A Division of CBS, Inc.
1107 Broadway
New York, New York 10010

Available at many major toy stores

Description:

Picking the ball up and turning it over results in a "message" floating up to the mystery window.

Developmental value:

- Turning the ball over to reveal the message elicits the movement of supination, as the forearm is rotated to the "palms up" position.

Photo courtesy of
Schwartz Public Relations
Associates, Inc. for
Ideal®/CBS Toys

Magna Doodle® Magnetic Drawing Toy

Available from:

Ideal®
CBS Toys, A Division of CBS Inc.
1107 Broadway
New York, New York 10010

Available at many major toy stores

Description:

A magnetic sketch box. Moving the erase bar across the screen erases the picture so that a new one can be created.

Developmental value:

- Holding and using the pencil promotes the use of dynamic tripod grasp needed for handwriting skills.
- Creating pictures improves visual space and form perception.

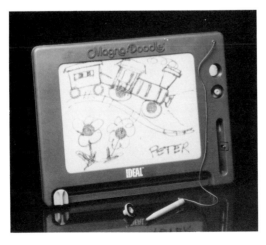

Photo courtesy of
Schwartz Public Relations
Associates, Inc. for
Ideal®/CBS Toys

MAGNASTIKS™

Available from:

Childcraft® Education Corporation
20 Kilmer Road
Edison, New Jersey 08818

Available through the Childcraft® catalog

Description:

Sculptures and figures are built and arranged on the magnetic tray surface by using and combining over ninety assorted pieces.

Developmental value:

- Picking up the pieces develops pincer grasp.
- Removing the pieces from the magnetic tray strengthens pincer grasp.
- Arranging the pieces to form figures and sculptures promotes the creative use of form and space perception.

Photo courtesy of
Childcraft®

MICKEY MOUSE TALKING PHONE

Available from:

Hasbro Bradley Industries, Inc.
1027 Newport Avenue
P.O. Box 1059
Pawtucket, Rhode Island 02862-1059

Available at many major toy stores

Description:

Turning the knob enables the child to choose one of six Disney characters; pressing the touch-tone numbers lets him or her hear Disney characters.

Developmental value:

- Turning the knob elicits and enhances pincer grasp ability.
- Pressing one of the buttons develops isolated finger use.

Disney Characters©
Walt Disney Productions

Photo courtesy of
Hasbro Bradley, Inc.

MIGHTY MOTOR BOATS®

Available from:

Tomy Corporation
901 East 233 Street
P.O. Box 6252
Carson, California 90749

Available at many major toy stores

Description:

Boats with wind-up motors.

Developmental value:

- Winding up the boat requires and develops a pincer grasp.

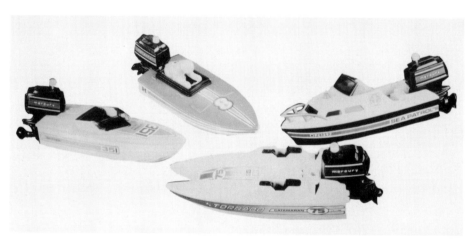

Photo courtesy of
Tomy Corp.

Mop top hair shop™ playset

Available from:

Kenner®
A subsidiary of General Mills, Inc.
1014 Vine Street
Cincinnati, Ohio 45202

Available at many major toy stores

Description:

After the characters are filled with Play-Doh®, they "grow" hair which can be styled or trimmed.

Developmental value:

- Turning the base of the chair around and around to cause the hair to "grow" enhances hand grasp and wrist rotation.
- Filling the characters with Play-Doh® strengthens finger muscles.
- Cutting the hair develops the ability to use a scissors.
- Feeling the hair provides tactile stimulation.
- Using the comb, scissors, or styling mold promotes motor planning and general manipulative skills.

Photo courtesy of
Kenner

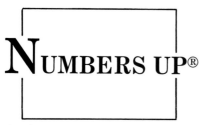

NUMBERS UP®

Available from:

Milton Bradley Company
443 Shaker Road
East Longmeadow, Massachusetts 01028-5247
Available at many major toy stores

Description:

One or more players race against the clock to unscramble the twenty numbered pegs and arrange them in numerical order before the timer runs out.

Developmental value:

- Picking up the pegs and placing them in the holes provides an opportunity to practice pincer grasp and release.
- Quickly manipulating the pegs improves fine-motor dexterity.
- Placing the pegs into the holes enhances eye-hand coordination.
- Putting the numbered pegs into the proper order develops counting skills.

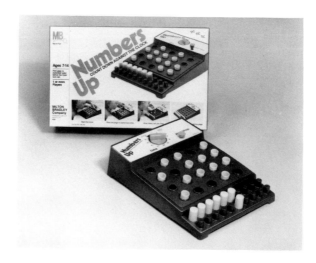

Photo courtesy of
Milton Bradley Co.

 OH CHUTE!

Available from:

Schaper® Manufacturing Company
P.O. Box 1426
Minneapolis, Minnesota 55440

Available at many major toy stores

Description:

Two players take turns dropping discs down the chute, trying to get three discs of the same color in a row, horizontally, vertically, or diagonally. The players can also move one of the horizontal slides one hole to either side, causing a disc to fall out of the frame.

Developmental value:

- Picking up the discs and dropping them down the chutes provides an opportunity to practice pincer grasp and release.
- Dropping the discs into the chutes improves eye-hand coordination.

Photo courtesy of
Schaper® Mfg. Co.

OPERATION®

Available from:

Milton Bradley Company
443 Shaker Road
East Longmeadow, Massachusetts 01028-5247

Available at many major toy stores

Description:

One or more players "operate" on the patient by removing the plastic ailment with a pair of tweezers. The buzzer sounds and the patient's red nose lights up if the "doctor" slips.

Developmental value:

- Using the tweezers requires and utilizes a pincer grasp.
- Removing the plastic ailments without hitting the walls of the cavity improves eye-hand coordination and motor planning.

Photo courtesy of
Milton Bradley Co.

THE PAST PLANES® COLLECTION

Available from:

Tomy Corporation
901 East 233 Street
P.O. Box 6252
Carson, California 90749

Available at many major toy stores

Description:

Antique planes that taxi down the runway and spin their propellers when wound up.

Developmental value:

- Winding up the toys requires and develops pincer grasp.

Photo courtesy of
Tomy Corp.

Plasticine® BARREL OF FUN™

Available from:

Colorforms®

Ramsey, New Jersey 07446

Available at many major toy stores

Description:

Modeling material that never hardens or dries out.

Developmental value:

- Squeezing the clay can improve grasp and pinch strength.
- Manipulating the clay provides tactile and kinesthetic input, and helps develop motor planning.

Photo courtesy of
Colorforms®

POCKET PETS®

Available from:

Tomy Corporation
901 East 233 Street
P.O. Box 6252
Carson, California 90749

Available at many major toy stores

Description:

Animals that hop, waddle, or walk when wound up.

Developmental value:

- Winding up the toys requires and develops pincer grasp.

Photo courtesy of
Tomy Corp.

POPOIDS™ COSMIC CONCERT™

Available from:

Tomy Corporation
901 East 233 Street
P.O. Box 6252
Carson, California 90749

Available at many major toy stores

Description:

A seven-piece set which can be used in various combinations to create unique instruments.

Developmental value:

- Pressing down on the keys promotes isolated finger function.
- Connecting the pieces together to form an instrument requires bilateral and eye-hand coordination.

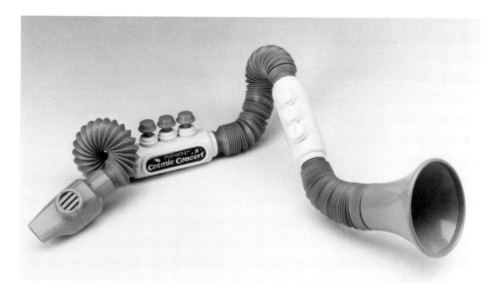

Photo courtesy of
Tomy Corp.

PUFF-PUSH

Available from:

Achievement Products® Inc.
P.O. Box 547
Mineola, New York 11501
Available through Achievement Products® catalog

Description:

One to four children guard their goals by squeezing the puff and letting the air push the opponent's ping pong ball away.

Developmental value:

- Squeezing the puff strengthens hand grasp.

Photo courtesy of
Achievement Products®

PUSH 'N POP® PHONE

Available from:

Tomy Corporation
901 East 233 Street
P.O. Box 6252
Carson, California 90749

Available at many major toy stores

Description:

When the correct buttons which correspond to a "phone number" are pushed down, a picture pops up.

Developmental value:

- Pressing the buttons develops isolated finger function, particularly of the extended index finger.

Photo courtesy of
Tomy Corp.

REBOUND® GAME

Available from:

Ideal®
CBS Toys, A Division of CBS Inc.
1107 Broadway
New York, New York 10010

Available at many major toy stores

Description:

A compact shuffleboard game. The puck is pushed down the alley and rebounds off the cushions into the scoring area.

Developmental value:

- Pushing the pucks down the alley promotes isolated finger function (i.e. of the extended index finger).
- Picking up the pucks requires and develops pincer grasp.
- Aiming a puck to knock an opponent's puck out of the scoring area improves eye-hand coordination.

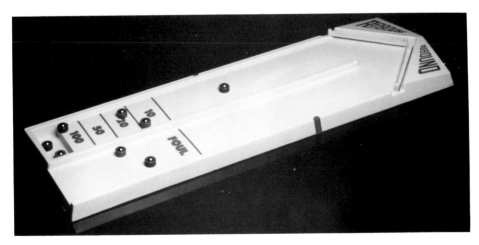

Photo courtesy of
Schwartz Public Relations
Associates, Inc. for
Ideal®/CBS Toys

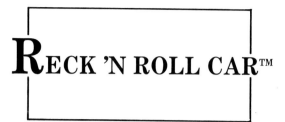RECK 'N ROLL CAR™

Available from:

Tomy Corporation
901 East 233 Street
P.O. Box 6252
Carson, California 90749

Available at many major toy stores

Description:

A high speed vehicle in which motor action is triggered by pulling backward on the car. When the car comes in contact with an obstacle, the front end will climb up that obstacle, then roll over and take off in another direction.

Developmental value:

- Pulling back on the car develops wrist extension.

Photo courtesy of
Tomy Corp.

 ROBO STRUX™

Available from:

Tomy Corporation
901 East 233 Street
P.O. Box 6252
Carson, California 90749

Available at many major toy stores

Description:

Fully motorized robot monsters which can be constructed and then activated.

Developmental value:

- Constructing the monster develops pincer grasp and general manipulative ability.

Photo courtesy of
Tomy Corp.

RUB N' PLAY™ TRANSFERS

Available from:

Colorforms®

Ramsey, New Jersey 07446

Available at many major toy stores

Description:

Transfers which can be rubbed onto a piece of paper.

Developmental value:

- Rubbing the transfers onto a piece of paper improves and strengthens the ability to grasp a writing instrument.

Pictured on left:
Robotman™, © 1984 UFS, Inc.

Pictured on right:
Pink Panther and Sons™, and
©1984 United Artists Corp.

All Rights Reserved.

Photo courtesy of
    Colorforms®

SCORE FOUR®

Available from:

Lakeside
495 Post Road East
Westport, Connecticut 06880

Available at many major toy stores

Description:

A three-dimensional tic tac toe game played vertically, horizontally, and diagonally. Two to four players try to score by placing the beads on the pins four in a row in any direction.

Developmental value:

- Picking up each bead requires and refines pincer grasp.
- Placing a bead on a pin improves eye-hand coordination.
- Planning which pin to place a bead on helps to develop visual perception and problem-solving strategy as the player needs to screen out extraneous visual stimuli (figure-ground perception) such as beads in other rows while focusing on those pins which are needed to complete a diagonal, vertical, or horizontal line (directionality).

Photo courtesy of
Gerald Freeman, Inc.
Public Relations for
Lakeside

SCURRY FURRIES®

Available from:

Tomy Corporation
901 East 233 Street
P.O. Box 6252
Carson, California 90749

Available at many major toy stores

Description:

Furry toys that hop when wound up.

Developmental value:

- Winding up the toys requires and develops a pincer grasp.
- Playing with the toys provides tactile stimulation.

Photo courtesy of
Tomy Corp.

SESAME STREET® BUSY POPPIN' PALS®

Available from:

Child Guidance®
CBS Toys, A Division of CBS Inc.
41 Madison Avenue
New York, New York 10010

Available at many major toy stores

Description:

A busy toy with five different activities: pushing, twirling, sliding, clicking, and turning.

Developmental value:

- Playing with the various devices improves general manipulative ability.

®Sesame Street Muppets, Muppets Inc.

Photo courtesy of
Schwartz Public Relations
Associates, Inc. for
Child Guidance®/CBS Toys

SESAME STREET® FINGER PUPPETS

Available from:

Child Guidance®
CBS Toys, A Division of CBS Inc.
41 Madison Avenue
New York, New York 10010

Available at many major toy stores

Description:

Finger puppets.

Developmental value:

•Playing with the puppets develops isolated finger function.

Sesame Street Muppets© Muppets, Inc.

Photo courtesy of
    Schwartz Public Relations
    Associates, Inc. for
    Child Guidance®/CBS Toys

SHUFFLETOWN SCHOOL™ PLAYSET

Available from:

Hasbro Bradley Industries, Inc.
1027 Newport Avenue
P.O. Box 1059
Pawtucket, Rhode Island 02862-1059

Available at many major toy stores

Description:

A playset with no loose pieces. Characters move by shuffling and sliding over the board.

Developmental value:

- Pushing the characters around the board improves reaching ability.
- Playing with the set (i.e. ringing the school bell, opening the doors and windows, and turning the flag pole around) enhances general manipulative skills.
- Moving the figures around the board promotes eye-hand coordination.

Photo courtesy of
Hasbro Bradley, Inc.

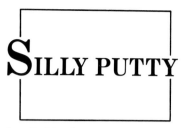

SILLY PUTTY

Available from:

Binney and Smith
1100 Church Lane
P.O. Box 431
Easton, Pennsylvania 18042

Available at many major toy stores

Description:

A putty with special qualities. It can be squeezed, rolled, broken apart, put back together, and used to pick up print from a newspaper.

Developmental value:

- Squeezing the putty can improve grasp strength.
- Squeezing a small ball of putty between the thumb and index finger or pulling off small bits of putty can improve pinch strength.
- Rolling out the putty into a long "snake" can enhance bilateral coordination.

Photo courtesy of
Binney and Smith

SKILL SQUARES™

Available from:

Tomy Corporation
901 East 233 Street
P.O. Box 6252
Carson, California 90749

Available at many major toy stores

Description:

Miniature action games such as Goin' Ape, Rocket Tower, Basketball, Shootin' Gallery, Rescue Copter, and Mini Mouth.

Developmental value:

- Pressing the lever to activate the balls develops the ability to isolate and use the extended index finger.
- Watching the movement of the balls promotes visual tracking skills.
- Playing the game enhances eye-hand coordination.

Photo courtesy of
Tomy Corp.

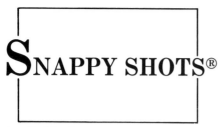 SNAPPY SHOTS®

Available from:

Tomy Corporation
901 East 233 Street
P.O. Box 6252
Carson, California 90749

Available at many major toy stores

Description:

A pretend camera which produces color "negatives."

Developmental value:

- Pressing the button to produce the "negative" promotes the isolated use of the index finger.
- Holding the camera in one hand while pressing the button or retrieving the negative with the other is a bimanual activity.

Photo courtesy of
Tomy Corp.

STAMP-A-SHAPE

Available from:

Lauri, Inc.
Phillips-Avon, Maine 04966
Available through many special education catalogs

Description:

Crepe foam rubber geometric and free-form shapes which can be used with stamp pads or water-soluble colors to stamp graphic designs onto paper.

Developmental value:

- Picking up and holding the shapes promotes a refined pincer grasp.
- Choosing which shapes to use and planning where to stamp them on the paper to create a design enhances visual perception of form and space.

Photo courtesy of
Lauri, Inc.

STAY ALIVE®

Available from:

Milton Bradley Company
443 Shaker Road
East Longmeadow, Massachusetts 01028-5247

Available at many major toy stores

Description:

Two to four players use strategy in maneuvering the plastic slides on the playing board in an attempt to open up the holes that will cause their opponent's marbles to drop through. The winner is the last player with marbles on the board.

Developmental value:

- Maneuvering the plastic slides develops isolated finger use.
- Picking up the marbles gives an opportunity to practice pincer grasp.

Photo courtesy of
Milton Bradley Co.

STELLAR™ AND ROBOTMAN™ STUFFED FIGURES

Available from:

Kenner®
A subsidiary of General Mills, Inc.
1014 Vine Street
Cincinnati, Ohio 45202

Available at many major toy stores

Description:

Musical toys whose hearts, when pressed, play a song.

Developmental value:

- Pressing the heart develops and strengthens the ability to isolate and use an extended index finger.

Photo courtesy of
Kenner

Stuff it!™

Available from:

Lakeside
495 Post Road East
Westport, Connecticut 06880
Available at many major toy stores

Description:

Foam figures are stuffed into the phone booth by two to four players. The player who causes the booth to pop open by squeezing too many of the foam shapes in through the windows is the loser.

Developmental value:

- Holding the foam shapes and then letting them go can improve the ability to grasp and release.
- Stuffing the foam figures in through the windows requires eye-hand coordination.

Photo courtesy of
Gerald Freeman, Inc.
Public Relations for
Lakeside

TALKING MICKEY MOUSE

Available from:

Child Guidance®
CBS Toys, A Division of CBS Inc.
41 Madison Avenue
New York, New York 10010

Available at many major toy stores

Description:

A plush toy who talks when his string is pulled.

Developmental value:

- Pulling the string requires and develops isolated finger function.

Disney Characters©
Walt Disney Productions

Photo courtesy of
Schwartz Public Relations
Associates, Inc. for
Child Guidance®/CBS Toys

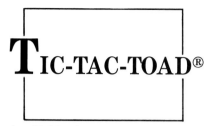 Tic-Tac-Toad®

Available from:

Synergistics Research Corporation
650 Avenue of the Americas
New York, New York 10011

Available at many major toy stores

Description:

The toad's tail is pushed down so that it jumps into the playboard. Three toads in a row wins.

Developmental value:

- Pushing the toad's tail down requires and develops the ability to use an extended index finger.
- Aiming the toad at the appropriate space improves eye-hand coordination.

Photo courtesy of
Synergistics Research Corp.

TINY FINGERS™

Available from:

Tomy Corporation
901 East 233 Street
P.O. Box 6252
Carson, California 90749

Available at many major toy stores

Description:

A radio, tape player, and record player which make clicking and ring-ing sounds, and feature moving pictures when the buttons are pushed or twisted.

Developmental value:

- Pushing or twisting the buttons encourages isolated finger func-tion.

Photo courtesy of
Tomy Corp.

TOMY® TUTOR PLAY COMPUTER™

Available from:

Tomy Corporation
901 East 233 Street
P.O. Box 6252
Carson, California 90749

Available at many major toy stores

Description:

A play computer with twelve different pictures which are animated by pushing the space bar.

Developmental value:

- Pressing one of the twelve keys develops isolated finger function.
- Aiming for and manipulating a specific key improves eye-hand coordination.

Photo courtesy of
Tomy Corp.

TRAVEL SHUT THE BOX™

Available from:

Milton Bradley Company
443 Shaker Road
East Longmeadow, Massachusetts 01028-5247

Available at many major toy stores

Description:

A pocked-sized strategy game for two or more players. Levers are pushed down in accordance with numbers rolled on dice. Players attempt to leave as few levers as possible for their opponents to push down. When no more levers can be pushed down, the game ends.

Developmental value:

- Pushing down the levers and keeping score on the sliding scale develops the ability to extend and isolate the index finger.
- Picking up the dice gives an opportunity to utilize pincer grasp.

Photo courtesy of
Milton Bradley Co.

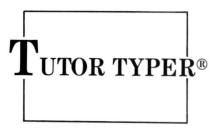

TUTOR TYPER®

Available from:

Tomy Corporation
901 East 233 Street
P.O. Box 6252
Carson, California 90749

Available at many major toy stores

Description:

A play typewriter which exhibits numbers and letters of the alphabet.

Developmental value:

- Pressing one of the number of alphabet keys develops isolated finger function.
- Aiming for and manipulating a specific key improves eye-hand coordination.

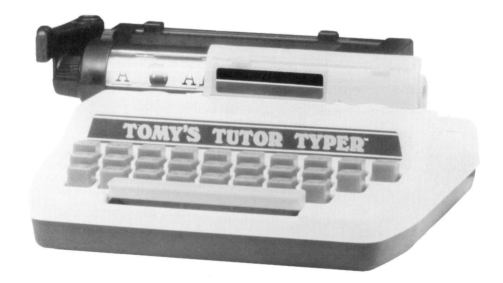

Photo courtesy of
Tomy Corp.

TWELVE TEEPEES MEMORY®

Available from:

Milton Bradley Company
443 Shaker Road
East Longmeadow, Massachusetts 01028-5247

Available at many major toy stores

Description:

Two to four players hide five Indian pawns under five teepees which are either empty or house opponents' Indians.

Developmental value:

- Picking up each teepee develops pincer grasp.
- Figuring out which are the correct hiding places requires and improves memory skills.

Photo courtesy of
Milton Bradley Co.

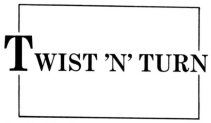

Twist 'N' Turn

Available from:

Achievement Products® Inc.
P.O. Box 547
Mineola, New York 11501
Available through Achievement Products® catalog

Description:

Three different shapes can be twisted and turned onto the rod.

Developmental value:

- Twisting and turning the shapes onto the rod develops forearm pronation and supination.
- Placing the shapes onto the rod improves eye-hand coordination and bilateral coordination.

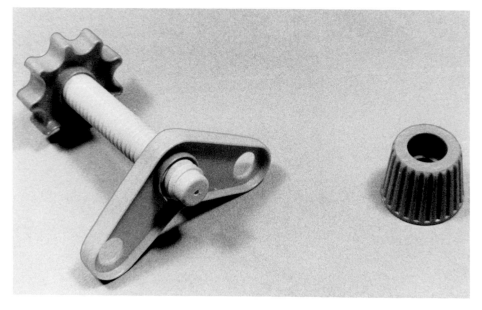

Photo courtesy of
Achievement Products®

WEE WONDERFUL WATERFULS®

Available from:

Tomy Corporation
901 East 233 Street
P.O. Box 6252
Carson, California 90749

Available at many major toy stores

Description:

Self-contained water games in which pressing the button propels tiny
balls or rings towards a target.

Developmental value:

- Pressing the button develops the ability to isolate and use the
  thumb or index finger.
- Visually following the movement of the balls or rings promotes visual tracking ability.

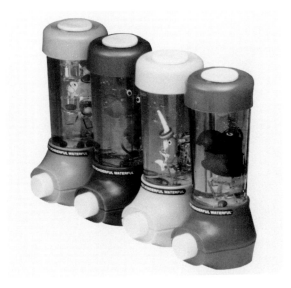

Photo courtesy of
Tomy Corp.

CHAPTER 3

SENSORY DEVELOPMENT

T HE MAJOR sensory functions (tactile, proprioceptive, kinesthetic, vestibular, auditory, and visual) are discussed in this chapter. The olfactory (sense of smell) and gustatory (sense of taste) functions are not included.

TACTILE FUNCTIONING

The sense of touch is an essential means of acquiring knowledge about the outside world. In addition to providing information about the external environment, tactile input also helps to formulate body awareness and aids in the development of motor planning.

PROPRIOCEPTION AND KINESTHESIA

Proprioception is the internal *nonconscious* awareness of the *position* of the body parts, whereas kinesthesia is a more *conscious* internal awareness of the *movement* of the body parts. Unlike tactile functioning, proprioceptive and kinesthetic information comes from internal stimuli within the body itself.

Both proprioception and kinesthesia contribute to all functional movement, including locomotion. They also contribute to the development of body awareness. When functioning optimally, they allow the child to move without needing to pay excessive visual and cognitive attention to the movement.

A vicious circle may occur when a child has not adequately developed the proprioceptive and kinesthetic senses, as is often the case when movement experiences have been limited. The inadequate kinesthesia leads to poor motor performance, and forces him or her to devote a great deal of visual attention to the activity and to work slowly to monitor the performance. He or she then may become less inclined and less motivated to participate in the motor experiences which are needed to develop kinesthesia.

VESTIBULAR FUNCTIONING

The vestibular system located in the nonauditory portion of the inner ear helps to maintain equilibrium and spatial orientation. Optimal functioning of the vestibular system enables the child to detect and adjust to changes in gravity and movement. In addition, vestibular input contributes to the development of motor planning, body awareness, and visual functioning.

AUDITORY FUNCTIONING

Perceiving and interpreting a sound stimulus is a crucial ability. The first developmental step is the awareness of sound and attending to the stimulus. This then enables discrimination to develop. The child learns to recognize and respond appropriately to similarities and differences in sounds, such as frequency, intensity, and duration.

Auditory memory is another crucial aspect of processing sound. The child needs to be able to remember the characteristics of a given sound. Sound sequencing, as the ability to identify a series of sounds in correct sequential order, is also extremely important and critical for the development of verbal language.

VISUAL FUNCTIONING

Visual functioning is crucial for all aspects of development, including gross-motor skills, fine-motor skills, perception, and cognition. Important visual processing abilities include visual awareness, tracking, and scanning. Unless the child can visually attend for an adequate length of time, he or she will be unable to develop advanced visual and cognitive skills. Tracking is important because it enables the child to smoothly follow a visual target without losing it or having to move the head. Scanning ability is essential because it allows the child to locate, discriminate, and match forms, patterns, and configurations at near point and far point.

The toys and games in this chapter can be utilized to enhance sensory development in one or more of the following areas:

- auditory discrimination
- auditory memory
- kinesthetic input
- proprioceptive input
- sound sequencing
- tactile discrimination
- tactile stimulation
- vestibular stimulation
- visual attention
- visual sequencing
- visual tracking

BEGINNER'S INDIVIDUAL JUMPER

Available from:

Achievement Products® Inc.
P.O. Box 547
Mineola, New York 11501

Available through Achievement Products® catalog

Description:

A dynamic jumper.

Developmental value:

- Bouncing on the jumper provides proprioceptive input.
- Jumping on the jumper improves bilateral coordination of the lower extremities, body awareness, and balance adjustments.

Photo courtesy of
Achievement Products®

CLOWN KALEIDOSCOPE

Available from:

Steven Manufacturing Company
224 East 4th Street
Hermann, Missouri 65041-0275

Available at many major toy stores

Description:

A kaleidoscope which is worked by twisting the clown's nose.

Developmental value:

- Viewing the designs through the viewing hole improves visual attention.
- Using the kaleidoscope is a two-handed activity, requiring the kaleidoscope to be held with one hand while the nose is twisted with the other.

Photo courtesy of
Steven Mfg. Co.

FEEL AND MATCH - TEXTURES

Available from:

Lauri, Inc.
Phillips-Avon, Maine 04966

Available through many special education catalogs

Description:

Six pairs of disks made of different textured materials such as felt, plastic, and rubber.

Developmental value:

- Feeling the disks in order to pair them with the other disk of the same texture provides an opportunity to develop and exercise tactile discrimination.

Photo courtesy of
Lauri, Inc.

LARGE COLORED BEADS AND PATTERNS

Available from:

Ideal School Supply Company
11000 South Lavergne Avenue
Oak Lawn, Illinois 60453

Available through the Ideal catalog

Description:

Beads of different shapes, laces, and cards with various sequences of the beads.

Developmental value:

- Following the sequence develops visual tracking and sequencing.
- Stringing the beads promotes bilateral coordination, eye-hand coordination, and pincer grasp.

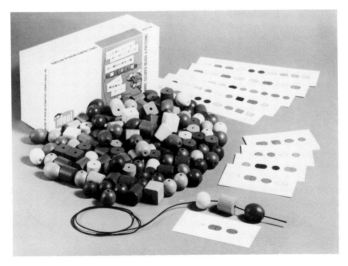

Photo courtesy of
Ideal School Supply Co.

LONG SQUISHY WALKING MAT

Available from:

Achievement Products® Inc.
P.O. Box 547
Mineola, New York 11501
Available through Achievement Products® catalog

Description:

A styrene bead path covered with vinyl, enabling the child to walk on it.

Developmental value:

- Walking on the uneven, crunchy surface provides kinesthetic and tactile input.
- Walking on the mat develops balance reactions.

Photo courtesy of
Achievement Products®

MULTI-SENSORY CUBES AND SPHERES

Available from:

Ideal School Supply Company
11000 South Lavergne Avenue
Oak Lawn, Illinois 60453

Available through the Ideal catalog

Description:

Twelve smooth and twelve rough textured cubes and spheres.

Developmental value:

- Sorting the cubes and spheres into categories of rough and smooth develops tactile discrimination.
- Sorting the cubes and spheres into categories of form, size, or color promotes visual perception of these qualities.

Photo courtesy of
Ideal School Supply Co.

Multi-Texture Puzzles

Available from:

Lauri, Inc.
Phillips-Avon, Maine 04966
Available through many special education catalogs

Description:

A textured puzzle in which the pieces which comprise the animals' bodies are made of artificial fur.

Developmental value:

- Manipulating the puzzle pieces provides tactile stimulation.
- Completing the puzzle provides an opportunity to develop visual perception of space and form.

Photo courtesy of
Lauri, Inc.

REDSKIN® FINGER PAINT

Available from:

Milton Bradley Company
443 Shaker Road
East Longmeadow, Massachusetts 01028-5247

Available at many major toy stores

Description:

Finger paints, paper, and spatulas.

Developmental value:

- Moving the hands in the finger paint provides tactile and kinesthetic input.

Photo courtesy of
Milton Bradley Co.

ROLL-A-BALL

Available from:

Achievement Products® Inc.
P.O. Box 547
Mineola, New York 11501
Available through Achievement Products® catalog

Description:

When the wooden balls are dropped in the hole on the top left, they descend down three ramps to the bottom.

Developmental value:

- Watching the balls move through the toy develops horizontal visual tracking.

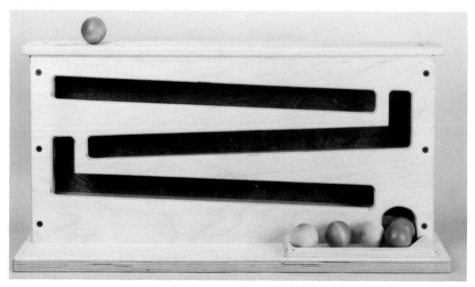

Photo courtesy of
Achievement Products®

Rub-a-dub® DOGGIE BATHLAND™

Available from:

Child Guidance®
CBS Toys, A Division of CBS Inc.
41 Madison Avenue
New York, New York 10010

Available at many major toy stores

Description:

A bathtub playset with two dogs who shake their heads, ride down a slide, and float on a "bone boat."

Developmental value:

- Playing in the water provides tactile stimulation.
- Using the ball to squirt at the bone and spinning water wheel moving targets strengthens hand grasp and improves eye-hand coordination.

Photo courtesy of
Schwartz Public Relations
Associates, Inc. for
Child Guidance®/CBS Toys

SAND AND WATER TABLE

Available from:

Ideal School Supply Company
11000 South Lavergne Avenue
Oak Lawn, Illinois 60453
Available through the Ideal catalog

Description:

A hardwood table for sand and/or water play.

Developmental value:

• Playing with sand or water provides tactile stimulation.

Photo courtesy of
Ideal School Supply Co.

SIMON®

Available from:

Milton Bradley Company
443 Shaker Road
East Longmeadow, Massachusetts 01028-5247

Available at many major toy stores

Description:

A game of concentration in which one or more players must repeat the exact sequences of colors and sounds that they have seen and heard from the machine.

Developmental value:

- Playing the game improves auditory discrimination, memory, and sound sequencing.
- Playing the game improves concentration and memory skills.

Photo courtesy of
Milton Bradley Co.

TEETER-FOR-TWO

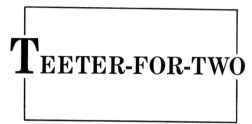

Available from:

The Little Tikes® Company
2180 Barlow Road
Hudson, Ohio 44236

Available at many major toy stores

Description:

A teeter-totter.

Developmental value:

- Rocking on the teeter-totter provides vestibular stimulation.
- Holding onto the handles incorporates the use of both hands.
- Using the teeter-totter promotes balance, motor planning, gross-motor coordination, and body awareness.

Photo courtesy of
the Little Tikes Co.

TEXTURE BOARD

Available from:

Achievement Products® Inc.
P.O. Box 547
Mineola, New York 11501

Available through Achievement Products® catalog

Description:

Children match the surfaces on the board with cylinder-shaped
wooden pieces of ten different textured and colored surfaces by using
either visual or tactile cues.

Developmental value:

- Matching the cylinders with the surfaces on the board without vision enhances tactile discrimination.
- Visually matching the cylinders with the surfaces on the board develops visual perception of color, texture, and design.
- Picking up the pieces and placing them into the hole improves hand grasp and release, as well as eye-hand coordination.

Photo courtesy of
Achievement Products®

TOMY® TUBBIES™

Available from:

Tomy Corporation
901 East 233 Street
P.O. Box 6252
Carson, California 90749

Available at many major toy stores

Description:

Bathtub toys which move their tails as they swim in water.

Developmental value:

- Playing with the toys in the water provides tactile stimulation.
- Winding up the toys requires and develops pincer grasp.

Photo courtesy of
Tomy Corp.

Touch and Tell

Available from:

Ideal School Supply Company
11000 South Lavergne Avenue
Oak Lawn, Illinois 60453

Available through the Ideal catalog

Description:

Twelve disks whose eight different textures (i.e. plastic, velvet, linen, silk, corduroy, wool, fine and coarse sandpaper) can be matched or described (i.e. smooth/rough).

Developmental value:

- Matching the texture of the circles promotes tactile discrimination.
- Feeling the textures provides tactile stimulation.

Photo courtesy of
Ideal School Supply Co.

Tubtown® MERRY-GO-ROUND

Available from:

Lakeside
495 Post Road East
Westport, Connecticut 06880

Available at many major toy stores

Description:

A floating carousel which spins when water is poured into the top with the Rainbow Scooper.

Developmental value:

- Playing with the carousel in the water provides tactile stimulation.
- Pouring the water into the top requires eye-hand coordination, as does placing the two Tubtown® people into their Turtle Floats or into their holes on the Merry-Go-Round.

Photo courtesy of
Gerald Freeman, Inc.
Public Relations for
Lakeside

TUBTOWN SEA CIRCUS®

Available from:

Lakeside
495 Post Road East
Westport, Connecticut 06880

Available at many major toy stores

Description:

Though this aquatic circus easily attaches to the side of a bathtub, it can also be used for out of tub play. Its many play features include slides, shoots, a diving board, hoop, and a whale that squirts.

Developmental value:

- Playing with the circus in the water provides tactile stimulation.
- Manipulating the dolphin into and around the slide, shoot, and hoops can improve eye-hand coordination.

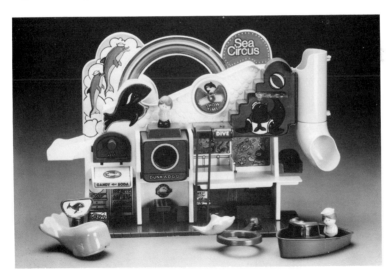

Photo courtesy of
Gerald Freeman, Inc.
Public Relations for
Lakeside

VISUAL TRACKING CARDS

Available from:

Ideal School Supply Company
11000 South Lavergne Avenue
Oak Lawn, Illinois 60453

Available through the Ideal catalog

Description:

Mark-on, wipe-off cards in which dots are connected by drawing a crayon line from one dot to another.

Developmental value:

• Connecting the dots develops visual tracking ability.

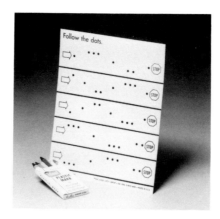

Photo courtesy of
Ideal School Supply Co.

CHAPTER 4

SENSORY-MOTOR DEVELOPMENT

SENSORY-MOTOR development can be viewed as a spiraling continuum in which sensory input results in motor ouput which, in turn, results in sensory feedback. The seven major areas of sensory-motor development are body awareness, visual-motor integration, motor planning, bilateral coordination, midline crossing, right-left discrimination, and postural/balance reactions. All these areas overlap one another and develop in conjunction with each other.

BODY AWARENESS

Body awareness is essential for the performance of many perceptual-motor tasks and self-care activities, in addition to being crucial for emotional development. The child needs to understand the location of his or her body parts and their relationship to one another in order to effectively utilize his or her body for functional activities.

Body awareness includes perceptual, linguistic, and conceptual elements. The development of these elements is aided by sensory input from visual, tactile, proprioceptive, kinesthetic, and vestibular stimuli.

Children whose movement experiences have been restricted in quantity and quality may show evidence of inadequate body awareness. This lack of gross-motor experiences may stem from motoric handicaps or simply a lack of opportunities within the environment to engage in movement activities.

VISUAL-MOTOR INTEGRATION

Coordination between visual input and motor output is a necessary prerequisite for many functional activities. Without adequate eye-hand or eye-foot coordination, performance of everyday activities such as feeding, dressing, writing, walking, and athletics is ineffective and inaccurate.

Visual-motor integration develops and becomes refined over a period of time as a result of repeated practice of activities which demand eye-hand or eye-foot coordination. Many children who lack optimal visual-motor skills do not have any motoric handicaps or visual deficits; instead, they seem to have an *integrative* problem in coordinating the visual and motor functions.

MOTOR PLANNING

Motor planning is the ability to plan and sequence movements which are essential to a nonhabitual, unique, and skilled activity. Without adequate motor planning, great difficulty is encountered in trying to learn new skills. The child is restricted to a very limited repertoire of motor skills and is forced to rely on the same few movements over and over again, even though these movements might not be efficient and successful in performing an activity.

Visual-motor integration also enables successful completion of motor activities, but it is an entirely different function than motor planning. The child with poor visual-motor integration knows what he or she wants to do and performs the necessary movements in the correct sequence but usually misses the target, whereas the child with poor motor planning can accurately reach the target of an activity which requires a simple visual-motor match but does not know how to plan and sequence more complex activities with varying steps and motions.

As is the case with body awareness, motor planning develops through sensory input (such as tactile, vestibular, proprioceptive, and kinesthetic stimuli) which provides feedback about motor performance. Among the many reasons why children may manifest impaired motor planning in gross-motor and fine-motor activities are: inadequate body awareness; impaired tactile, proprioceptive, kinesthetic, and vestibular functioning; and limited environmental opportunities to engage in a variety of sensory-motor activities.

BILATERAL COORDINATION

Integration of the two body sides is a necessary prerequisite for many gross- and fine-motor activities. The child who lacks the ability to coordinate the two upper or two lower extremities together will not be able to smoothly and effectively perform those activities which require simultaneous or reciprocal interaction between the two extremities. If the two body sides aren't adequately integrated, the development of body awareness, midline crossing, and right-left discrimination might be severely impeded.

The most basic level of bilateral coordination is awareness of the two body sides. The next step is the coordinated use of the two arms or two legs together. Once the two body sides can be used simultaneously in a parallel activity, the final developmental step is the ability to perform reciprocal movements in activities that contrast the body sides. This enables the child to participate in activities such as pedaling a bicycle or to engage one hand in a skilled activity while the other hand acts as an assist.

It should be noted that, in order to achieve good bilateral coordination, there must be adequate coordination in each of the extremities. A neuromuscular disorder which impairs muscle tone, strength, mobility, or coordination in one extremity will prevent optimal coordination between the two extremities, but this is to be distinguished from an *integrative* problem in which, although there is no neuromotor dysfunction in either extremity, the two arms or legs cannot be successfully coordinated. In the latter case, the poorly integrated bilateral function may be due to a communication problem between the brain's two hemispheres or simply to a lack of opportunities to engage in two-handed activities which develop bilateral integration.

MIDLINE CROSSING

The ability to use a body part, such as an arm, in the contralateral side of space develops from and contributes to body awareness, bilateral integration, laterality, and spatial orientation. The child who avoids crossing the midline and instead uses the right hand to manipulate objects on his or her right side and the left hand for objects on the left side will never develop a hand dominance. When dominance is not established, highly skilled fine-motor function cannot develop.

The developmental problem of not crossing the midline should not be confused with a physical inability to *ever* cross the body midline. In the latter case, limited shoulder or elbow function may prevent one or both of the arms from being utilized on the other side of the body. In the former case, it is an integrative deficit in which the child *tends* to use the right arm on the right side of the body and the left arm on the left side.

RIGHT-LEFT DISCRIMINATION

The ability to understand and use concepts of right and left develops as the child begins to use one hand more than the other and becomes aware of that hand as a left or right entity. Once the child understands that he or she has two body sides and can attach verbal labels to them, he or she can begin to develop concepts of laterality imposed on another person or on objects.

Right-left discrimination cannot develop without adequate body awareness and bilateral integration. Cognitive/language deficiencies can also impede the learning of the verbal labels of right and left on the self, on others, and on objects.

POSTURAL/BALANCE REACTIONS

Postural mechanisms are motor responses which enable the child to spontaneously adjust to changes in gravity or body position without losing his or her balance. Without this ability, children can be extremely awkward and afraid of movement.

The toys and games in this chapter can be utilized to enhance sensory-motor development in one or more of the following areas:

- balance and equilibrium reactions
- bilateral hand use
- bilateral coordination of the lower extremities
- body awareness
- eye-foot coordination
- eye-hand coordination
- gross-motor coordination
- midline crossing
- motor planning
- reciprocal coordination
- right-left discrimination

BALANCE DISK

Available from:

Ideal School Supply Company
11000 South Lavergne Avenue
Oak Lawn, Illinois 60453

Available through the Ideal catalog

Description:

A rigid platform that can be rocked in any predetermined direction or set in a circular motion.

Developmental value:

• Standing on the disk develops balance and equilibrium reactions.

Photo courtesy of
Ideal School Supply Co.

BARREL OF MONKEYS®

Available from:

Lakeside
495 Post Road East
Westport, Connecticut 06880

Available at many major toy stores

Description:

Plastic monkeys are linked arm-in-arm to make a chain. Any number can play. The object is to link as many monkeys together as possible.

Developmental value:

- Linking the monkeys together demands and improves eye-hand coordination.
- Trying to hook the monkeys together quickly can improve fine-motor dexterity.

Photo courtesy of
Gerald Freeman, Inc.
Public Relations for
Lakeside

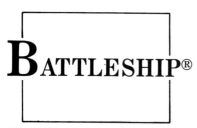

BATTLESHIP®

Available from:

Milton Bradley Company
443 Shaker Road
East Longmeadow, Massachusetts 01028-5247
Available at many major toy stores

Description:

A strategic game in which two players try to sink their opponent's ships by firing salvos of shots and calling out the strike area. Hit and misses are marked by pegs.

Developmental value:

- Inserting the pegs into the holes develops eye-hand coordination.
- Picking up and holding the pegs enhances pincer grasp.

Photo courtesy of
Milton Bradley Co.

Beads 'n Baubles

Available from:

Lauri, Inc.
Phillips-Avon, Maine 04966
Available through many special education catalogs

Description:

Crepe foam rubber pieces in various colors, shapes, and sizes with ¼″ diameter holes. Laces with tips are included.

Developmental value:

- Stringing the beads improves eye-hand coordination.
- Holding the beads in one hand while holding the lace and threading it through with the dominant hand requires and enhances bilateral hand use.
- Picking up and then letting go of the pieces enhances pincer grasp and release.

Photo courtesy of
Lauri, Inc.

BEANO BEAN BAG SET

Available from:

Ideal School Supply Company
11000 South Lavergne Avenue
Oak Lawn, Illinois 60453

Available through the Ideal catalog

Description:

A bean bag target set.

Developmental value:

- Aiming and throwing the bean bags improves eye-hand coordination.

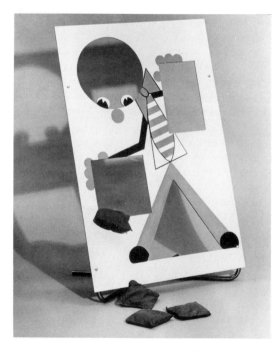

Photo courtesy of
Ideal School Supply Co.

BE BA BO IMAGE UNIT

Available from:

Ideal School Supply Company
11000 South Lavergne Avenue
Oak Lawn, Illinois 60453

Available through the Ideal catalog

Description:

A life-size child made of flannel body parts.

Developmental value:

- Placing the body parts on the boards promotes right-left discrimination and body awareness.

Photo courtesy of
Ideal School Supply Co.

BIG BIRD XYLOPHONE

Available from:

Child Guidance®
CBS Toys, A Division of CBS Inc.
41 Madison Avenue
New York, New York 10010

Available at many major toy stores

Description:

A brightly colored xylophone.

Developmental value:

- Hitting the keys with the mallet improves eye-hand coordination.
- Following a color-coded song in the songbook develops color matching skills.

Big Bird© Muppets Inc.

Photo courtesy of
  Schwartz Public Relations
  Associates, Inc. for
  Child Guidance®/CBS Toys

BIG BOUNCE

Available from:

G. Pierce Toy Company
P.O. Box 89
Skokie, Illinois 60077

Available at many major toy stores

Description:

An inflatable toy similar to a trampoline for bouncing.

Developmental value:

- Bouncing on the Big Bounce facilitates equilibrium and balance reactions.
- Jumping on the Big Bounce encourages bilateral coordination of the lower extremities.
- Bouncing on the Big Bounce provides proprioceptive input.

Photo courtesy of
G. Pierce Toy Co.

BODY PARTS PUZZLE

Available from:

Lauri, Inc.
Phillips-Avon, Maine 04966

Available through many special education catalogs

Description:

A crepe foam rubber puzzle in which the body part pieces conform to actual human joints. A lay-on assembly pattern and a sheet with nine possible poses are included.

Developmental value:

- Playing with the puzzle improves awareness of body parts.
- Arranging the pieces to match one of the poses on the sheet can contribute to the development of body awareness.

Photo courtesy of
Lauri, Inc.

"BOOM BOOM" STAND UP PUNCHING BAG

Available from:

G. Pierce Toy Company
P.O. Box 89
Skokie, Illinois 60077

Available at many major toy stores

Description:

A punching bag on a stand.

Developmental value:

- Hitting the bag promotes reciprocal coordination between the arms.
- Punching the bag can improve arm strength.

Photo courtesy of
G. Pierce Toy Co.

BUILD A BETTER BURGER®

Available from:

Lakeside
495 Post Road East
Westport, Connecticut 06880

Available at many major toy stores

Description:

Two to four players try to build a burger and complete their menus from over 100 food parts (such as hamburgers, pickles, lettuce, ketchup, mustard, french fries, milk shakes, and pies) as the burger tower revolves.

Developmental value:

- Reaching for the various ingredients and stacking them promotes eye-hand coordination.
- Picking up the food parts can help refine pincer grasp and release.
- Completing the menu while the menu card revolves on the burger tower improves visual memory and form perception.

Photo courtesy of
Gerald Freeman, Inc.
Public Relations for
Lakeside

Burger King* Whopper* Sandwich Stacking Game

Available from:

Tomy Corporation
901 East 233 Street
P.O. Box 6252
Carson, California 90749

Available at many major toy stores

Description:

A stacking game in which the ingredients of a Whopper* sandwich are stacked on top of each other. Up to four players compete against each other, taking turns to place an ingredient on the stack. If a piece falls off, the player must keep that piece and try to stack it on another turn. The first player to place his or her last piece on the stack and balance the top bun on the sandwich is the winner.

Developmental value:

- Stacking one ingredient on top of another develops eye-hand coordination.

Photo courtesy of Tomy Corp.

*Whopper and Burger King are registered trademarks of Burger King Corp.

CHILDCRAFT® SPACE WHEELS

Available from:

Childcraft® Education Corporation
20 Kilmer Road
Edison, New Jersey 08818
Available through the Childcraft® catalog

Description:

A construction set of large transparent polystyrene pieces. Each piece has nine connection slots along its circumference.

Developmental value:

- Connecting the pieces demands the use of both hands together, as the nondominant hand holds the base piece and the dominant hand connects the new piece to the structure.
- Inserting one piece into the connection slot of another improves eye-hand coordination, motor planning, and space perception.

Photo courtesy of
Childcraft®

CLIP-CLOP® THE WONDER HORSE®

Available from:

Wonder®
CBS Toys, A Division of CBS Toys
41 Madison Avenue
New York, New York 10010

Available at many major toy stores

Description:

A spring horse with five motion-activated electronic sounds.

Developmental value:

- Riding the horse improves balance and equilibrium reactions.

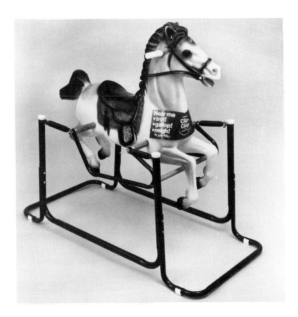

Photo courtesy of
Schwartz Public Relations
Associates, Inc. for
Wonder®/CBS Toys

COBBLER'S BENCH

Available from:

Playskool®, Inc.
A Hasbro Bradley Company
1027 Newport Avenue
Pawtucket, Rhode Island 02862

Available at many major toy stores

Description:

Six pegs are pounded into the wooden bench.

Developmental value:

- Hitting the pegs requires and improves eye-hand coordination.
- Using pressure on the mallet can improve hand strength.

Photo courtesy of
Playskool®, Inc.

COOTIE™

Available from:

Schaper® Manufacturing Company
P.O. Box 1426
Minneapolis, Minnesota 55440

Available at many major toy stores

Description:

Players compete to be the first to assemble their Cootie® bug. The roll of the dice determines which body parts can be utilized.

Developmental value:

• Assembling the Cootie™ bug enhances general manipulative skills and eye-hand coordination.

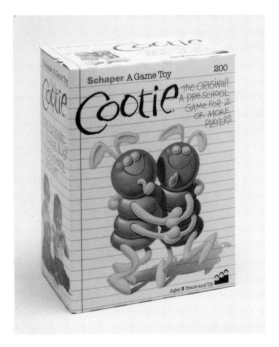

Photo courtesy of
Schaper® Mfg. Co.

DELUXE ROCKER BALANCE SQUARE

Available from:

Achievement Products® Inc.
P.O. Box 547
Mineola, New York 11501
Available through Achievement Products® catalog

Description:

A rocking platform made of wood and covered with carpet.

Developmental value:

- Sitting, kneeling, or standing on the balance square develops balance and equilibrium reactions.

Photo courtesy of
Achievement Products®

DON'T BREAK THE ICE®

Available from:

Schaper® Manufacturing Company
P.O. Box 1426
Minneapolis, Minnesota 55440

Available at many major toy stores

Description:

One to four players take turns tapping out the blocks of "ice" with a mallet, while trying not to let the Iceman fall through the ice. The winner is the last player left after all the others have caused the Iceman to fall through the ice.

Developmental value:

- Tapping out the ice with mallet improves eye-hand coordination.
- Planning which block of ice to tap out provides an opportunity to develop strategy based on perceptions of spatial relations.

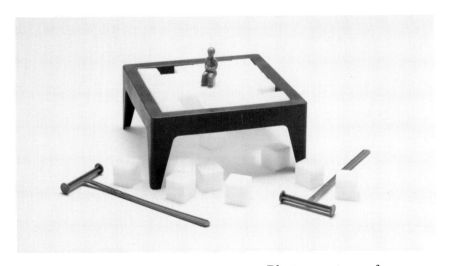

Photo courtesy of
Schaper® Mfg. Co.

DRIVE 'N PLAY™ CONSOLE

Available from:

Child Guidance®
CBS Toys, A Division of CBS Inc.
41 Madison Avenue
New York, New York 10010

Available at many major toy stores

Description:

The car is steered through and around roadway obstacles, using the "throttle" to control the driving direction.

Developmental value:

- Steering the wheel with one hand while operating the throttle with the other develops the ability to use the two hands in contrasting motions.
- Manipulating the throttle promotes active wrist extension.
- Steering the car through and around roadway obstacles improves visual space perception and motor planning.

Photo courtesy of
Schwartz Public Relations
Associates, Inc. for
Child Guidance®/CBS Toys

EARLY YEARS LADDER

Available from:

Achievement Products® Inc.

P.O. Box 547

Mineola, New York 11501

Available through Achievement Products® catalog

Description:

A playground ladder for climbing.

Developmental value:

- Climbing on the ladder develops bilateral coordination of the arms and legs, motor planning, and body spatial awareness.
- Hanging on the ladder and moving from one bar to the next with just the arms improves arm strength.

Photo courtesy of
Achievement Products®

ERECTOR® CONSTRUCTION SYSTEM

Available from:

Ideal®
CBS Toys, A Division of CBS Inc.
1107 Broadway
New York, New York 10010

Available at many major toy stores

Description:

A steel girder construction system. Includes tools and step-by-step building plans.

Developmental value:

- Assembling a structure enhances eye-hand coordination.
- Connecting two pieces requires and improves bilateral coordination.
- Using the tools can improve motor planning.
- Following the building plan helps to develop visual space and form perception, as well as sequencing, direction-following, and other cognitive skills.

Photo courtesy of
Schwartz Public Relations
Associates, Inc. for
Ideal®/CBS Toys

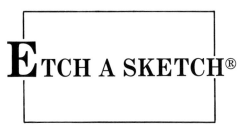

ETCH A SKETCH®

Available from:

Ohio Art Company
P.O. Box 111
Bryan, Ohio 43506

Available at many major toy stores

Description:

Turning the left knob produces horizontal lines on the "magic" screen; vertical lines are drawn by turning the right knob. Curved lines are created by turning the knobs simultaneously. The picture can be erased by shaking the screen. Plastic overlays are available which fit onto the magic screen. These overlays contain games, puzzles, mazes, and other drawing activities.

Developmental value:

- Using the two dials to draw lines enhances bilateral coordination.
- Grasping the dials requires and develops pincer grasp.
- Moving the dials to create pictures improves motor planning.
- Creating a design improves visual space and form perception.

Photo courtesy of
Ohio Art Co.

FISHER-PRICE BUBBLE MOWER

Available from:

Fisher-Price
Division of the Quaker Oats Company
636 Girard Avenue
East Aurora, New York 14052-1885

Available at many major toy stores

Description:

A lawn-mower which makes bubbles as it is pushed along.

Developmental value:

- Pushing the mower is a two-handed activity which develops bilateral coordination.
- Operating the pretend sound lever with ratchet sound and the ignition key that clicks improves pincer grasp ability.

Photo courtesy of
Fisher-Price

Foam hockey set

Available from:

Achievement Products® Inc.
P.O. Box 547
Mineola, New York 11501

Available through Achievement Products® catalog

Description:

Because this hockey set is made of foam, it will not injure children if accidentally hit during play.

Developmental value:

- Using the hockey stick to hit the puck towards a goal improves eye-hand coordination.
- Holding the hockey stick requires the use of two hands.
- Hitting the puck with the stick towards the goal encourages elbow extension.

Photo courtesy of
Achievement Products®

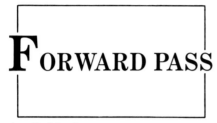

FORWARD PASS

Available from:

DLM Teaching Resources
One DLM Park
Allen, Texas 75002

Available through the DLM Teaching Resources catalog

Description:

A ball on a rope which is passed from one player to another by moving the handles quickly apart.

Developmental value:

- Sending the ball to the other player by moving the handles apart requires bilateral coordination.
- Pulling the handles apart is a resistive activity which improves upper extremity strength.
- Knowing when to send the ball back requires depth perception and eye-hand coordination.

Photo courtesy of
DLM Teaching Resources

GARFIELD© GIANT BALL DARTS®

Available from:

Synergistics Research Corporation
650 Avenue of the Americas
New York, New York 10011

Available at many major toy stores

Description:

Two Velcro®-covered balls are thrown at the target.

Developmental value:

* Aiming the balls at the numbered targets improves eye-hand coordination.

Garfield and Odie© 1978
United Feature Syndicate, Inc.

Photo courtesy of
  Synergistics Research Corp.

GEO-DOME

Available from:

Achievement Products® Inc.
P.O. Box 547
Mineola, New York 11501

Available through Achievement Products® catalog

Description:

A climber.

Developmental value:

- Climbing on the Geo-Dome develops motor planning, spatial relations, and gross-motor coordination.

Photo courtesy of
Achievement Products®

GET IN SHAPE, GIRL!™ RHYTHM AND RIBBONS™

Available from:

Hasbro Bradley Industries, Inc.
1027 Newport Avenue
P.O. Box 1059
Pawtucket, Rhode Island 02862-1059

Available at many major toy stores

Description:

A ribbon attached to a stick. Includes a cassette tape with music and instructions on rhythmic gymnastics.

Developmental value:

- Performing rhythmic ribbon movements such as "serpents" or "figure eights" improves eye-hand or eye-foot coordination.
- Performing the movements develops general gross-motor coordination.
- Performing many of the movements will necessitate crossing the body midline.

Photo courtesy of
Hasbro Bradley, Inc.

GIGGLE GANG™

Available from:

Lakeside
495 Post Road East
Westport, Connecticut 06880

Available at many major toy stores

Description:

Four fabric toys in the shape of a banana, strawberry, peanut, and donut. Each toy comes with a variety of interchangeable facial features which attach to the figure with Velcro®. Hundreds of different faces are possible.

Developmental value:

- Planning where to place a facial feature such as the eyes or mouth can enhance body awareness.
- Placing the facial features on the figure improves fine-motor dexterity.
- Removing the facial features from the figure in order to change the face can strengthen pincer grasp as the Velcro® is pulled away from the fabric.

Photo courtesy of
Gerald Freeman, Inc.
Public Relations for
Lakeside

HACKY SACK® FOOTBAG

Available from:

Wham-O®, Inc.
835 East El Monte Street
P.O. Box 4
San Gabriel, California 91778-0004

Available at many major toy stores

Description:

A leather footbag which is kept in the air through foot movements.

Developmental value:

- Keeping the ball in the air develops eye-foot coordination.

Photo courtesy of
Wham-O®

HAPPY SOUND™ TOOLS

Available from:

Tomy Corporation
901 East 233 Street
P.O. Box 6252
Carson, California 90749

Available at many major toy stores

Description:

Hammering the nail, turning the screw, and twisting the bolt produces unique sound effects.

Developmental value:

- Manipulating the fasteners with the tools promotes eye-hand coordination.
- Turning the screw and twisting the bolt develops motor planning.
- Matching the tools with the fasteners enhances color perception.

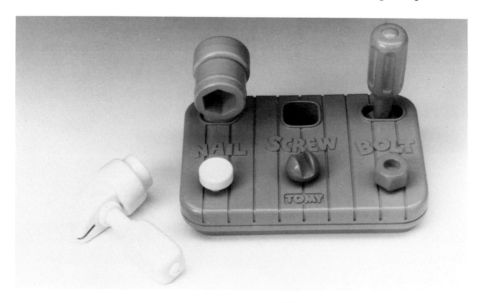

Photo courtesy of
Tomy Corp.

HARMON WALKING RAIL

Available from:

Ideal School Supply Company
11000 South Lavergne Avenue
Oak Lawn, Illinois 60453

Available through the Ideal catalog

Description:

A walking rail which slopes outward and downward from the center to each side.

Developmental value:

- Walking on the rail improves walking balance.

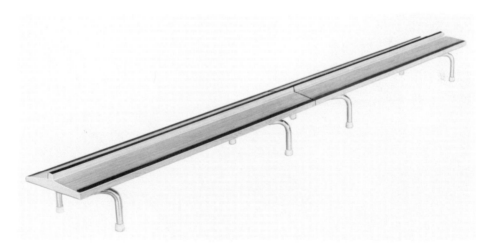

Photo courtesy of
Ideal School Supply Co.

INDOOR/OUTDOOR SHUFFLEBOARD

Available from:

Achievement Products® Inc.
P.O. Box 547
Mineola, New York 11501

Available through Achievement Products® catalog

Description:

A plastic court with four cues, four yellow discs, and four black discs.

Developmental value:

- Aiming the discs towards the numbered target areas improves eye-hand coordination.
- Pushing the discs with the cues develops shoulder range of motion and mobility, as well as elbow extension.

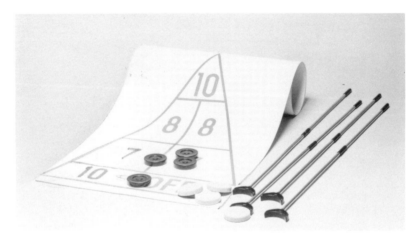

Photo courtesy of
Achievement Products®

JUMP BOARD

Available from:

Ideal School Supply Company
11000 South Lavergne Avenue
Oak Lawn, Illinois 60453

Available through the Ideal catalog

Description:

A hardwood jumping board.

Developmental value:

- Jumping off the board improves bilateral coordination of the lower extremities.

Photo courtesy of
Ideal School Supply Co.

KABOOMERS® INDOOR/OUTDOOR PADDLE GAME

Available from:

Ideal®
CBS Toys, A Division of CBS Inc.
1107 Broadway
New York, New York 10010
Available at many major toy stores

Description:

An inflatable paddle with a pump in the middle. These air-powered paddles have a "trampoline" effect when they contact with the ball, causing it to really fly.

Developmental value:

- Hitting the soft foam ball with the paddle improves eye-hand coordination.
- Squeezing the handles to inflate the paddles to playing size can strengthen finger muscles and hand grasp.

Photo courtesy of
Schwartz Public Relations
Associates, Inc. for
Ideal®/CBS Toys

KITTY IN THE KEGS™

Available from:

Child Guidance®
CBS Toys, A Division of CBS Inc.
41 Madison Avenue
New York, New York 10010

Available at many major toy stores

Description:

Five kegs are opened to reveal a kitten in the smallest.

Developmental value:

- Opening the kegs is a two-handed activity which improves bilateral coordination.
- Placing the kegs right side up on the table encourages forearm supination.
- Putting the kegs together develops color and size perception.

Photo courtesy of
Schwartz Public Relations
Associates, Inc. for
Child Guidance®/CBS Toys

Lace-A-Puppet

Available from:

Lauri, Inc.
Phillips-Avon, Maine 04966
Available through many special education catalogs

Description:

Felt puppets with holes for lacing. The kit includes needles, yarn, and colorful decorative shapes to cut and glue.

Developmental value:

- Inserting the yarn through the holes improves eye-hand coordination.
- Grasping the needle, yarn, or decorative shapes promotes the use of a pincer grasp.

Photo courtesy of
Lauri, Inc.

LACING SHAPES

Available from:

Lauri, Inc.
Phillips-Avon, Maine 04966
Available through many special education catalogs

Description:

Colorful shapes with holes for lacing. Non-kink laces are included.

Developmental value:

- Inserting the lace through the holes improves eye-hand coordination.
- Grasping the pieces or the lace promotes the use of a pincer grasp.

Photo courtesy of
Lauri, Inc.

LACING SOLDIER

Available from:

Achievement Products® Inc.
P.O. Box 547
Mineola, New York 11501

Available through Achievement Products® catalog

Description:

The soldier is laced so that his head and legs stay together. Gold lace decorates his uniform and the lacing needle becomes his rifle.

Developmental value:

- Lacing the soldier improves eye-hand coordination and motor planning.

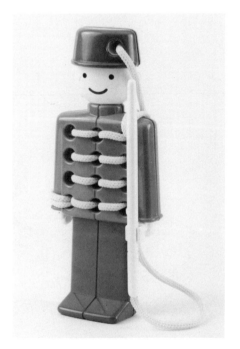

Photo courtesy of
Achievement Products®

LARGE ABACUS

Available from:

DLM Teaching Resources
One DLM Park
Allen, Texas 75002

Available through the DLM Teaching Resources catalog

Description:

A counting frame with one hundred beads in ten rows.

Developmental value:

- Pushing a bead from one side to another with one hand promotes midline crossing.
- Grasping a bead requires and develops pincer grasp ability.
- Utilizing the abacus teaches mathematical skills of counting, adding, and subtracting.

Photo courtesy of
DLM Teaching Resources

LEARNING TOWER™

Available from:

Child Guidance®
CBS Toys, A Division of CBS Inc.
41 Madison Avenue
New York, New York 10010

Available at many major toy stores

Description:

   Twelve cups that stack on top of each other.

Developmental value:

- Stacking one cup on top of another improves eye-hand coordination.
- Matching the cups in terms of size or color improves color and size perception.

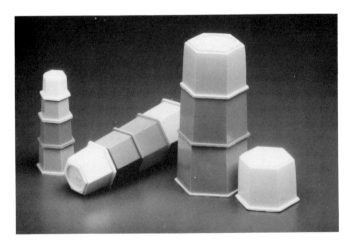

Photo courtesy of
   Schwartz Public Relations
   Associates, Inc. for
   Child Guidance®/CBS Toys

LITTLE DRIVER'S DASHBOARD®

Available from:

Tomy Corporation
901 East 233 Street
P.O. Box 6252
Carson, California 90749

Available at many major toy stores

Description:

A small dashboard with working features such as a horn, gear shift, rear view mirror, and windshield.

Developmental value:

- Steering the wheel while shifting or operating some of the other features requires coordination between the two upper extremities.
- Operating the controls helps to improve general manipulative skills.

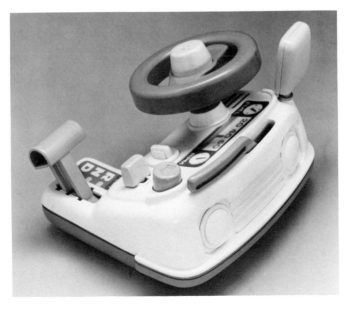

Photo courtesy of
Tomy Corp.

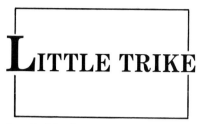

LITTLE TRIKE

Available from:

The Little Tikes® Company
2180 Barlow Road
Hudson, Ohio 44236

Available at many major toy stores

Description:

A tricycle with special safety and comfort features, such as a closed front wheel cover for added safety, foam handle grips for added comfort, and unique styling for extra leg room.

Developmental value:

- Pedaling the tricycle and holding on to the handles develops bilateral coordination of the lower and upper extremities.

Photo courtesy of
the Little Tikes Co.

LOCKTAGONS

Available from:

Lauri, Inc.
Phillips-Avon, Maine 04966

Available through many special education catalogs

Description:

Crepe foam rubber slotted, octagon-shaped wafers which fit together to form an infinite number of different kinds of structures.

Developmental value:

- Fitting the wafers together improves eye-hand coordination.
- Connecting one wafer with another requires a certain amount of bilateral coordination, since the nondominant hand needs to hold the base wafer while the dominant hand fits in the new wafer.
- Fitting together or pulling apart the wafers can improve pinch or grasp strength, as the light friction fit provides slight resistance.

Photo courtesy of
Lauri, Inc.

LOLLIPOP PADDLES SET

Available from:

Achievement Products® Inc.
P.O. Box 547
Mineola, New York 11501

Available through Achievement Products® catalog

Description:

Discs with handles that are used to hit lightweight balls.

Developmental value:

- Hitting balls with the paddles improves eye-hand coordination.

Photo courtesy of
Achievement Products®

MAGNETIC PIC-UP STIX

Available from:

Steven Manufacturing Company
224 East 4th Street
Hermann, Missouri 65041-0275

Available at many major toy stores

Description:

Pick-up sticks with a steel band around the middle and a magnetic "Magic Wand."

Developmental value:

- Picking up one stick at a time without moving the others by touching the steel bands with the Magic Wand improves eye-hand coordination.
- Grasping the Magic Wand requires and enhances pincer grasp.
- Selecting a stick which is on top and won't cause the others to move develops visual figure-ground discrimination and space perception.

Photo courtesy of
Steven Mfg. Co.

Mr. MOUTH®

Available from:

Tomy Corporation
901 East 233 Street
P.O. Box 6252
Carson, California 90749

Available at many major toy stores

Description:

A battery-operated toy in which one to four players try to toss their chips into the mouth as the head revolves and opens.

Developmental value:

- Flipping the chips into the mouth at the appropriate time improves eye-hand coordination.
- Pressing down on the lever to propel the chips into the mouth develops the ability to use the index finger in an isolated manner.

Photo courtesy of
Tomy Corp.

Mr. POTATO HEAD® FAMILY

Available from:

Hasbro Bradley, Inc.
1027 Newport Avenue
P.O. Box 1059
Pawtucket, Rhode Island 02862-1059

Available at many major toy stores

Description:

Potato bodies with bendable arms and interchangeable facial parts and accessories.

Developmental value:

- Placing facial features appropriately onto the bodies develops body awareness.
- Inserting the facial parts and accessories onto the body enhances eye-hand coordination.

Photo courtesy of
Hasbro Bradley, Inc.

NHL STANLEY CUP PLAY-OFF HOCKEY

Available from:

Coleco Industries, Inc.
999 Quaker Lane South
West Hartford, Connecticut 06110

Available at many major toy stores

Description:

A rod game which simulates pro hockey action.

Developmental value:

- Aiming the pucks towards the plastic netted goals to score develops eye-hand coordination.
- Manipulating more than one rod at a time promotes bilateral coordination.

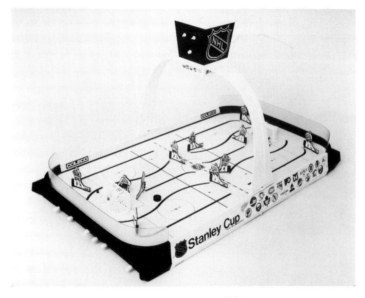

Photo courtesy of
Coleco Industries

Nuts 'n Bolts™

Available from:

Child Guidance®
CBS Toys, A Division of CBS Inc.
41 Madison Avenue
New York, New York 10010

Available at many major toy stores

Description:

Twenty nuts and bolts which fit together by color and size.

Developmental value:

- Screwing and unscrewing the nuts and bolts is a two-handed activity which improves bilateral coordination.
- Screwing and unscrewing the nuts and bolts encourages forearm supination.
- Matching the nuts to the bolts develops color and size perception.

Photo courtesy of
Schwartz Public Relations
Associates, Inc. for
Child Guidance®/CBS Toys

OFFICIAL "BOOM BOOM" BOP BAG

Available from:

G. Pierce Toy Company
P.O. Box 89
Skokie, Illinois 60077

Available at many major toy stores

Description:

An inflatable knock-down toy.

Developmental value:

- Hitting the bag promotes reciprocal coordination between the two arms.

Photo courtesy of
G. Pierce Toy Co.

ONE DOZEN COUNTING EGGS™

Available from:

Child Guidance®
CBS Toys, A Division of CBS Inc.
41 Madison Avenue
New York, New York 10010

Available at many major toy stores

Description:

A dozen eggs which can be opened up into two pieces, one of which has pegs and the other with holes, numbering from one to twelve.

Developmental value:

- Putting the pieces together is a two-handed activity which improves bilateral coordination.
- Matching the holes and pegs together improves counting skills.

Photo courtesy of
Schwartz Public Relations
Associates, Inc. for
Child Guidance®/CBS Toys

ONE-LEGGED BALANCE STOOL

Available from:

Achievement Products® Inc.
P.O. Box 547
Mineola, New York 11501
Available through Achievement Products® catalog

Description:

An adjustable height stool with a single leg.

Developmental value:

- Sitting on the stool develops balance reactions and forward/
  backward/lateral postural adjustments.

Photo courtesy of
Achievement Products®

PAC-MAN™ MAGNETIC MAZE™

Available from:

Tomy Corporation
901 East 233 Street
P.O. Box 6252
Carson, California 90749

Available at many major toy stores

Description:

A joy stick maneuvers Pac-Man™ through the maze. Along the way, he tries to pick up the magnetic pieces and escape the monster.

Developmental value:

- Manipulating the joy stick to maneuver Pac-Man™ through the maze develops eye-hand coordination and motor planning.
- Maneuvering Pac-Man™ through the maze improves space perception and directionality concepts.

Pac-Man© Bally
Midway Mfg. Co.

Photo courtesy of
Tomy Corp.

PAUL BUNYAN GIANT WOODEN STIX

Available from:

Steven Manufacturing Company
224 East 4th Street
Hermann, Missouri 65041-0275

Available at many major toy stores

Description:

Wooden pick-up sticks.

Developmental value:

- Picking up one stick at a time without moving the others improves eye-hand coordination.
- Grasping the stick requires and enhances pincer grasp.
- Selecting a stick which is on top and won't cause the others to move develops visual figure-ground discrimination and space perception.

Photo courtesy of
Steven Mfg. Co.

PEG-A-CAR

Available from:

Lauri, Inc.
Phillips-Avon, Maine 04966
Available through many special education catalogs

Description:

Crepe foam rubber shapes which are connected by wooden dowels according to full-size lay-on patterns.

Developmental value:

- Connecting the shapes together by inserting the dowels into the holes improves eye-hand coordination.
- Holding the shapes in one hand while inserting the dowels through the holes with the other hand requires bilateral coordination.
- Matching the shapes to the patterns helps to develop form perception.

Photo courtesy of
Lauri, Inc.

PEPPERMINT HULA HOOP®

Available from:

Wham-O®, Inc.
835 East El Monte Street
P.O. Box 4
San Gabriel, California 91778-0004

Available at many major toy stores

Description:

A plastic hoop which is set in motion by twisting the body.

Developmental value:

- Starting and keeping the hoop in motion promotes motor planning, body awareness, and balance adjustments.

Photo courtesy of
Wham-O®

PLASTIC HOOPS AND HOOP HOLDERS

Available from:

Achievement Products® Inc.
P.O. Box 547
Mineola, New York 11501

Available through Achievement Products® catalog

Description:

The hoop holders hold hoops either vertically or horizontally, allowing children to crawl or step through, around, or over the hoops.

Developmental value:

- Maneuvering the body in various relationships to the hoops develops body spatial awareness and motor planning.

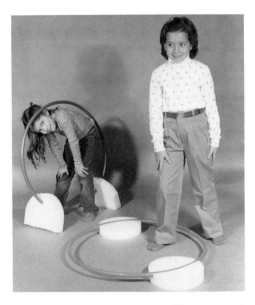

Photo courtesy of
Achievement Products®

Popoids™ COSMIC CRACKBOT™ SET

Available from:

Tomy Corporation
901 East 233 Street
P.O. Box 6252
Carson, California 90749

Available at many major toy stores

Description:

A construction set which lends itself to creating unique outer-space creatures.

Developmental value:

- Connecting the parts together promotes bilateral coordination as the nondominant hand holds one piece while the dominant hand inserts the other.
- Connecting the parts together requires eye-hand coordination.
- Creating a cosmic creature challenges visual space and form perception.

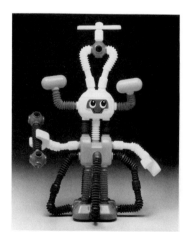

Photo courtesy of
Tomy Corp.

POWER JET™ HOCKEY

Available from:

Coleco Industries, Inc.
999 Quaker Lane South
West Hartford, Connecticut 06110

Available at many major toy stores

Description:

A hockey game with motorized air power for fast-paced action

Developmental value:

- Aiming and trying to get the puck into the goal zone develops eye-hand coordination.
- Using one arm to chase the puck in various positions across the board promotes midline crossing.

Photo courtesy of
Coleco Industries

Rainbow chain™

Available from:

Child Guidance®
CBS Toys, A Division of CBS Inc.
41 Madison Avenue
New York, New York 10010

Available at many major toy stores

Description:

Links of five different shapes and four colors.

Developmental value:

- Hooking the links together is a two-handed activity which improves bilateral coordination.
- Hooking the links together enhances eye-hand coordination.

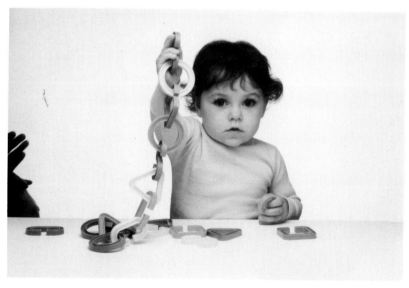

Photo courtesy of
Schwartz Public Relations
Associates, Inc. for
Child Guidance®/CBS Toys

RAINBOW STACKER™

Available from:

Lakeside
495 Post Road East
Westport, Connecticut 06880

Available at many major toy stores

Description:

Taking apart the rainbow results in a blue car/sailboat, a green three-piece puzzle, a yellow staircase and slide, and a red bridge.

Developmental value:

- Putting the rainbow together requires eye-hand coordination.
- Putting the rainbow together improves visual perception of size.

Photo courtesy of
Gerald Freeman, Inc.
Public Relations
for Lakeside

 Ring toss

Available from:

Lauri, Inc.
Phillips-Avon, Maine 04966
Available through many special education catalogs

Description:

Crepe foam rubber rings which are tossed onto a wooden dowel.

Developmental value:

- Aiming and tossing the rings onto the dowel enhances eye-hand coordination.
- Tossing the ring towards the target requires wrist extension.

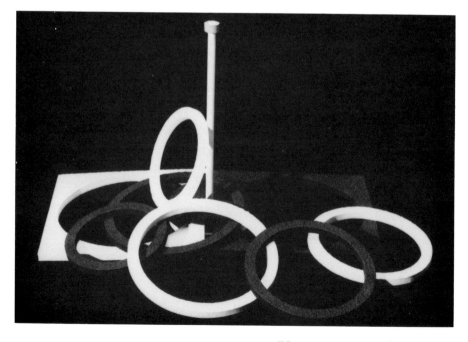

Photo courtesy of
Lauri, Inc.

ROMPER STOMPERS®

Available from:

Playskool®, Inc.
A Hasbro Bradley Company
1027 Newport Avenue
Pawtucket, Rhode Island 02862

Available at many major toy stores

Description:

Plastic cups which children stand on while grasping the handles.

Developmental value:

- Walking with the Romper Stompers® develops balance and equilibrium reactions.
- Walking around an obstacle course while on the Romper Stompers® can improve eye-foot coordination.

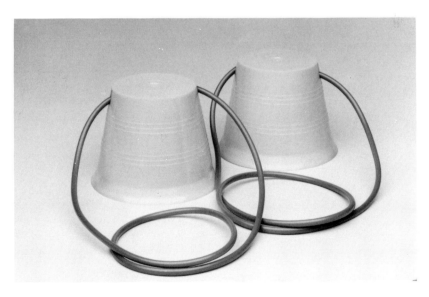

Photo courtesy of
Playskool®, Inc.

SESAME STREET® TRAVELING BAND™

Available from:

Child Guidance®
CBS Toys, A Division of CBS Inc.
41 Madison Avenue
New York, New York 10010

Available at many major toy stores

Description:

Five rhythm instruments.

Developmental value:

- Playing the drums, cymbals, and triangle is a two-handed activity which improves bilateral coordination.

Sesame Street Muppets
©Muppets, Inc.

Photo courtesy of
    Schwartz Public Relations
    Associates, Inc. for
    Child Guidance®/CBS Toys

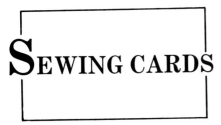

SEWING CARDS

Available from:

Colorforms®
Ramsey, New Jersey 07446
Available at many major toy stores

Description:

Sewing cards which are laced with yarn.

Developmental value:

- Inserting the yarn into the holes develops eye-hand coordination.
- Correctly lacing the card promotes directionality concepts of front and back.
- Holding the yarn develops pincer grasp.
- Following the holes improves visual tracking.

Pictured on left:
Muppet Babies™,
©1984 Henson Associates, Inc.

Pictured on right:
Wuzzles™
©1984 Hasbro Bradley, Inc.
– Walt Disney Productions

All Rights Reserved.
Photo courtesy of
    Colorforms®

SNAP-LOCK® BEADS

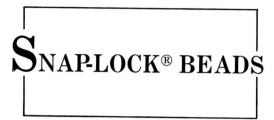

Available from:

Fisher-Price
Division of the Quaker Oats Company
636 Girard Avenue
East Aurora, New York 14052-1885

Available at many major toy stores

Description:

Plastic beads which are snapped together.

Developmental value:

- Connecting the beads or pulling them apart is a two-handed activity which improves bilateral coordination.
- Pushing the beads together or pulling them apart is a slightly resistive activity which can strengthen the arm muscles.

Photo courtesy of
Fisher-Price

Sno-Jet™

Available from:

Coleco Industries, Inc.
999 Quaker Lane South
West Hartford, Connecticut 06110

Available at many major toy stores

Description:

A snow coaster.

Developmental value:

- Riding on the coaster promotes sitting balance and develops equilibrium reactions.

Photo courtesy of
Coleco Industries

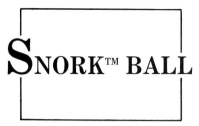

SNORK™ BALL

Available from:

Tomy Corporation
901 East 233 Street
P.O. Box 6252
Carson, California 90749

Available at many major toy stores

Description:

A catch game for one or two players. The characters' spring activated arms shoot the purple ball into the other snorkel.

Developmental value:

• Playing catch with the toy develops eye-hand coordination.

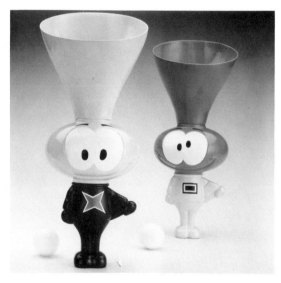

Snorks™ ©1985 SEPP
Licensed by Wallace Berrie

Photo courtesy of
    Tomy Corporation

SPIN AROUND CLOWNS™

Available from:

Lakeside
495 Post Road East
Westport, Connecticut 06880

Available at many major toy stores

Description:

Five clowns are stacked on the base according to size. Then, by lifting the first clown, and letting it go, all the clowns spin around.

Developmental value:

- Stacking the clowns onto the base requires eye-hand coordination.
- Stacking the clowns properly on the base demands and improves visual perception of size.

Photo courtesy of
Gerald Freeman, Inc.
Public Relations for
Lakeside

SPRING BRIDGES

Available from:

Achievement Products® Inc.
P.O. Box 547
Mineola, New York 11501
Available through Achievement Products® catalog

Description:

Walking beams which rest on four "squishy" wood and foam bases.

Developmental value:

- Walking on the gently moving surface challenges balance and equilibrium reactions.
- Moving the body along the beam develops motor planning and body spatial awareness.

Photo courtesy of
Achievement Products®

STACK 'N' TUMBLE CLOWNS™

Available from:

Lakeside
495 Post Road East
Westport, Connecticut 06880

Available at many major toy stores

Description:

A stacking toy in which five clowns are stacked and then made to
tumble down when tumblers are set on the highest clown.

Developmental value:

- Stacking the clowns requires and improves eye-hand coordination.
- Placing one clown on top of another can be aided by the nondominant hand acting as an assist, thus enhancing bilateral coordination.
- Counting skills can be learned through stacking the clowns which
  are numbered from one to five.

Photo courtesy of
Gerald Freeman, Inc.
Public Relations for
Lakeside

 STACROBATS

Available from:

Lauri, Inc.
Phillips-Avon, Maine 04966

Available through many special education catalogs

Description:

Crepe foam rubber pieces that fit together and balance in various ways.

Developmental value:

- Fitting the pieces together and balancing them necessitates eye-hand coordination.
- Placing stacrobats of the same color on top of each other can help to develop color perception.

Photo courtesy of
Lauri, Inc.

STENCIL SET

Available from:

Avalon Industries, Inc.
95 Lorimer Street
Brooklyn, New York 11206

Available at many major toy stores

Description:

A kit with plastic stencils, markers, crayons, and paint in no-mess, dripless applicator bottles.

Developmental value:

- Using the paint, markers, and crayons to stencil and color in the scenes promotes eye-hand coordination.
- Creating pictures with the stencils develops space and form perception.
- Tracing around the stencils provides kinesthetic input.

Photo courtesy of
Avalon Industries

STRINGING WOOD BEADS

Available from:

Playskool®, Inc.
A Hasbro Bradley Company
1027 Newport Avenue
Pawtucket, Rhode Island 02862

Available at many major toy stores

Description:

Wood beads in four different shapes and four colors.

Developmental value:

- Holding the string with one hand while stringing a bead with the dominant hand improves bilateral coordination.
- Stringing the beads enhances eye-hand coordination.

Photo courtesy of
Playskool®, Inc.

STUFF YER FACE™

Available from:

Milton Bradley Company
443 Shaker Road
East Longmeadow, Massachusetts 01028-5247

Available at many major toy stores

Description:

Two players scoop marbles from the tray with the arms of their clowns, trying to swallow as many as possible.

Developmental value:

- Scooping up the marbles with the arms of the clowns improves bilateral coordination, since the player's two arms must work together in moving the clown's two arms.
- Rotating the clown's arms to the "palms up" position to raise the marble to the mouth develops the ability to supinate the forearms.
- Bringing the marble up to the clown's mouth enhances eye-hand coordination.

Photo courtesy of
Milton Bradley Co.

SUPER JUMP POGO STICK

Available from:

G. Pierce Toy Company
P.O. Box 89
Skokie, Illinois 60077
Available at many major toy stores

Description:

A pogo stick.

Developmental value:

- Using the Super Jump Pogo Stick promotes equilibrium and balance reactions.
- Using the Super Jump Pogo Stick encourages the bilateral use of the arms and legs.
- Jumping while on the pogo stick provides proprioceptive input.

Photo courtesy of
G. Pierce Toy Co.

TABLE TOPPERS™ STUNT PILOT

Available from:

Tomy Corporation
901 East 233 Street
P.O. Box 6252
Carson, California 90749

Available at many major toy stores

Description:

The bi-plane or helicopter can perform such stunts as flying forward and reverse, picking up cargo, navigating an obstacle course, and landing safely.

Developmental value:

- Using the two controls (altitude stick and directional stick) promotes bilateral coordination.
- Controlling the plane to pick up cargo, navigate an obstacle course, and land safely develops eye-hand coordination.
- Using the small knob to wind-up the plane and helicopter helps to refine pincer grasp.

Photo courtesy of
Tomy Corp.

TAKE-APART WORKBENCH

Available from:

Playskool®, Inc.
A Hasbro Bradley Company
1027 Newport Avenue
Pawtucket, Rhode Island 02862

Available at many major toy stores

Description:

A workbench and tools such as a wrench, screwdriver, claw hammer, as well as pegs, nuts, and bolts.

Developmental value:

- Using the tools with the hammer improves eye-hand coordination and motor planning.

Photo courtesy of
Playskool®, Inc.

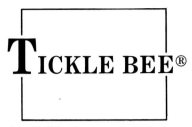

TICKLE BEE®

Available from:

Schaper® Manufacturing Company
P.O. Box 1426
Minneapolis, Minnesota 55440

Available at many major toy stores

Description:

The magnetic tickler takes the bee through the maze and back to his hive.

Developmental value:

- Taking the bee through the maze improves eye-hand coordination.
- Holding the magnetic tickler develops and improves the ability to grasp a writing instrument.

Photo courtesy of
Schaper® Manufacturing Co.

TINKERTOY® BUILDING SETS

Available from:

Child Guidance®
CBS Toys, A Division of CBS Inc.
41 Madison Avenue
New York, New York 10010

Available at many major toy stores

Description:

Construction toy with a variety of shapes.

Developmental value:

- Connecting the pieces together improves bilateral and eye-hand coordination.
- Creating a structure develops space and form perception.

Photo courtesy of
Schwartz Public Relations
Associates, Inc. for
Child Guidance®/CBS Toys

TRACKING ASSOCIATION CARDS

Available from:

DLM Teaching Resources
One DLM Park
Allen, Texas 75002
Available through the DLM Teaching Resources catalog

Description:

Laminated cards with intertwined paths, requiring the child to trace a path from the starting point to the finish.

Developmental value:

- Drawing a line within the track develops eye-hand coordination.
- Locating the most direct path improves figure-ground perception and tracking ability.

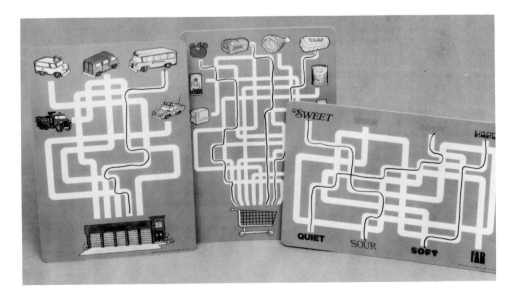

Photo courtesy of
DLM Teaching Resources

TUNNEL OF FUN

Available from:

G. Pierce Toy Company
P.O. Box 89
Skokie, Illinois 60077

Available at many major toy stores

Description:

A collapsible, crawl-through tunnel.

Developmental value:

• Crawling through the tunnel develops motor planning and body-spatial awareness.

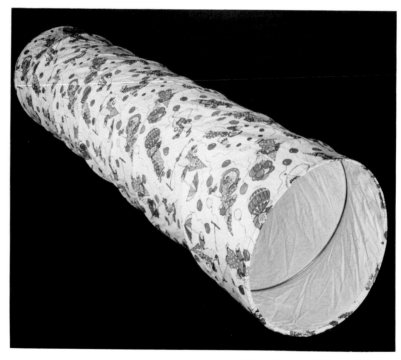

Photo courtesy of
G. Pierce Toy Co.

Turnin' Turbo Dashboard™

Available from:

Tomy Corporation
901 East 233 Street
P.O. Box 6252
Carson, California 90749

Available at many major toy stores

Description:

A dashboard with working features such as a four-speed gear shift and ignition key. The digital viewing screen lights up while the motor hums, to give the feel of actual movement behind the wheel.

Developmental value:

- Steering the wheel with two hands or with one hand while shifting with the other requires coordination between the two upper extremities.

Photo courtesy of
Tomy Corp.

Twister®

Available from:

Milton Bradley Company
443 Shaker Road
East Longmeadow, Massachusetts 01028-5247

Available at many major toy stores

Description:

Two to four players move a designated hand or foot into a different colored circle on the vinyl game rug. The last player to maintain his or her balance is the winner.

Developmental value:

- Maintaining many of the postures improves balance skills.
- Moving the correct arm and leg develops right/left discrimination.
- Moving into the various positions enhances motor planning and body awareness.
- Many of the required movements necessitate crossing the body midline.
- Playing the game can improve color perception.

Photo courtesy of
Milton Bradley Co.

WALT DISNEY© MINI GOLF

Available from:

HG Industries, Inc.
750 Park Place
Long Beach, New York 11561
Available at many major toy stores

Description:

A miniature golf set which can be played indoors or outside.

Developmental value:

- Hitting the golf ball towards the target improves eye-hand coordination.
- Holding and moving the golf club with two hands promotes bilateral coordination.

©Walt Disney Productions

Photo courtesy of
HG Industries

WOODEN FOOT PLACEMENT LADDER

Available from:

Achievement Products® Inc.
P.O. Box 547
Mineola, New York 11501
Available through Achievement Products® catalog

Description:

A ladder placed on the floor adjustable cross bars for different length steps and various walking patterns.

Developmental value:

- Walking through the ladder develops eye-foot coordination, depth perception, motor planning, and reciprocal gait patterns.

Photo courtesy of
Achievement Products®

WUZZLES™ BEAN BAG GAME

Available from:

Synergistics Research Corporation
650 Avenue of the Americas
New York, New York 10011

Available at many major toy stores

Description:

A fabric playboard with three bean bags that stick to the board with a Velcro® tab.

Developmental value:

- Aiming the bean bags at the numbered targets improves eye-hand coordination.

©1984 Hasbro Bradley, Inc.
Walt Disney Productions
All rights reserved.

Photo courtesy of
Synergistics Research Corp.

WUZZLES™ COLOR N' PLAY™

Available from:

Colorforms®
Ramsey, New Jersey 07446

Available at many major toy stores

Description:

Different scenes are colored with crayons, then decorated with the Colorforms® plastic Wuzzles™ figures that stick onto the picture.

Developmental value:

- Coloring within the lines improves eye-hand coordination and fine-motor accuracy.
- Coloring the pictures develops the ability to grasp a writing instrument.
- Decorating the picture with the Colorforms® plastic Wuzzles™ enhances space perception, as the figures are placed in appropriate spatial positions.

©1984 Hasbro Bradley, Inc.
Walt Disney Productions
All Rights reserved.

Photo courtesy of
    Colorforms®

CHAPTER 5

Visual-Perceptual Development

T HERE ARE several different but overlapping components of visual perception. All have important implications for the development of functional and academic skills.

FORM PERCEPTION

The ability to recognize and categorize forms and shapes is a basic perceptual ability. It first develops as the recognition of three-dimensional forms. The next developmental step is the recognition of two-dimensional pictorial representations of the three-dimensional objects; this allows geometric form discrimination to develop. The final step is perception of the constancy of forms, even in the presence of differing colors, textures, sizes, and spatial orientations. Though the extrinsic qualities may change, the form remains constant. A circle is still a circle, whether large or small, black or white, rough or smooth.

SPACE PERCEPTION

The most basic level of space perception is the awareness of the distance and direction of objects in relationship to one's own body. The child begins to learn the concepts of in-out, up-down, front-back, and far-near, even before he or she learns the verbal labels of spatial positions. This then enables the application of these concepts to external objects outside of the self. At its highest level, space perception enables the individual to visually perceive the position of one object to another without actually physically manipulating the objects.

Adequate space perception is a crucial prerequisite for many activities. If space perception is deficient, pre-academic and academic skills will be impaired. The child may be unable to organize space when writing his or her name and may instead scatter the letters haphazardly all over the page. Reading problems may also result. Difficulties with dressing can be another byproduct of impaired space perception. Clothing may be put on backwards or inside out and buttons may be aligned improperly. Language concepts of space, such as under, over, back, front, top, and bottom may not be mastered. The child may even have difficulty relating his or her body to other objects in the environment, particularly while moving, and may bump into doors, tables, or other people.

FIGURE-GROUND PERCEPTION

Adequate figure-ground perception enables the child to select and attend to one specific stimulus while keeping the majority of the competing stimuli in the background. Instead of being distracted by irrelevant details in the background, he or she is able to focus most of the visual attention on the main element in the foreground.

Other visual-perceptual skills include:

- size perception
- color perception
- depth perception

The toys and games in this chapter can be utilized to enhance visual-perceptual development in one or more of the following areas:

- color perception
- depth perception
- figure-ground perception
- form perception
- size perception
- space perception

ATTRIBUTE BLOCKS

Available from:

Ideal School Supply Company
11000 South Lavergne Avenue
Oak Lawn, Illinois 60453

Available through the Ideal catalog

Description:

Blocks with four distinct sets of attributes: five different shapes, three colors, two sizes, and two thicknesses.

Developmental value:

• Sorting the blocks develops visual perception of form, color, and size.

Photo courtesy of
Ideal School Supply Co.

COLORED INCH CUBES, DESIGNS, AND DESIGNS IN PERSPECTIVE

Available from:

DLM Teaching Resources
One DLM Park
Allen, Texas 75002

Available through the DLM Teaching Resources catalog

Description:

Hardwood cubes and design cards.

Developmental value:

- Copying a design develops space perception.
- Stacking one cube on top of another improves eye-hand coordination.

Photo courtesy of
DLM Teaching Resources

Cookie Monster Shape Muncher®

Available from:

Playskool®, Inc.
A Hasbro Bradley Company
1027 Newport Avenue
Pawtucket, Rhode Island 02862

Available at many major toy stores

Description:

Five bright shapes are dropped into their matching holes.

Developmental value:

- Fitting the shapes into their matching holes develops form perception.

Cookie Monster
©1985 MUPPETS, Inc.

Photo courtesy of
Playskool®, Inc.

CRAYOLA® LITTLE DESIGN MACHINE

Available from:

Binney and Smith
1100 Church Lane
P.O. Box 431
Easton, Pennsylvania 18042

Available at many major toy stores

Description:

The vertical movement of the machine is combined with the horizontal movement of the plastic tracing shapes to build pictures from basic geometric forms.

Developmental value:

- Planning the vertical and horizontal movements to produce a design develops space and form perception.
- Using crayons to trace the templates improves eye-hand coordination.

Photo courtesy of
Binney and Smith

DESIGN BLOCKS AND PATTERNS

Available from:

Ideal School Supply Company
11000 South Lavergne Avenue
Oak Lawn, Illinois 60453

Available through the Ideal catalog

Description:

Nine green and white one-inch cubes, each side of which is solid white, solid green, or half white and green. The blocks are arranged to match the patterns on the design cards.

Developmental value:

- Arranging the cubes to match the design cards enhances visual space and form perception.

Photo courtesy of
Ideal School Supply Co.

FIT-A-SPACE

Available from:

Lauri, Inc.
Phillips-Avon, Maine 04966

Available through many special education catalogs

Description:

Crepe foam rubber disks, each with three fit-in shapes such as
squares, rectangles, triangles, circles, ovals, diamonds, hearts, and
stars.

Developmental value:

- Matching the geometric shapes to the appropriate hole in the disks
  develops form perception.
- Matching the colors of the shapes and the disks improves color perception.

Photo courtesy of
Lauri, Inc.

FIT-IN PERCEPTION PUZZLES

Available from:

Lauri, Inc.
Phillips-Avon, Maine 04966
Available through many special education catalogs

Description:

Crepe foam rubber pieces of similar objects which fit into a rubber frame.

Developmental value:

Working the puzzle improves space and form perception.

NOTE: While all puzzles exercise visual perception, these puzzles are especially helpful because many of the differences between the puzzle pieces are quite subtle, requiring the child to attend to details.

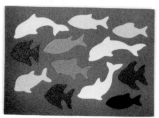

Pictured: Kids
Pictured: School of Fish
Photos courtesy of
Lauri, Inc.

FORM FITTER™

Available from:

Child Guidance®
CBS Toys, A Division of CBS Inc.
41 Madison Avenue
New York, New York 10010

Available at many major toy stores

Description:

Eighteen different shapes which fit only the corresponding holes in the cube.

Developmental value:

- Matching the shapes with their openings develops visual form perception.
- Inserting the shapes into the cube improves grasping ability and eye-hand coordination.

Photo courtesy of
Schwartz Public Relations
Associates, Inc. for
Child Guidance®/CBS Toys

FORMSET PUZZLES

Available from:

Ideal School Supply Company
11000 South Lavergne Avenue
Oak Lawn, Illinois 60453

Available through the Ideal catalog

Description:

Five-piece wood puzzles with knobs.

Developmental value:

- Placing the pieces into the correct holes develops size perception.
- Holding the piece by the knob develops pincer grasp.

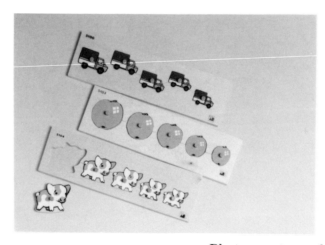

Photo courtesy of
Ideal School Supply Co.

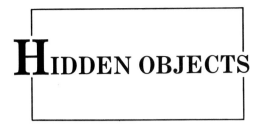

Available from:

Ideal School Supply Company
11000 South Lavergne Avenue
Oak Lawn, Illinois 60453
Available through the Ideal catalog

Description:

Cards on which objects are hidden within the scene.

Developmental value:

- Finding the hidden objects develops figure-ground perception.

Photo courtesy of
Ideal School Supply Co.

KEYS OF LEARNING™

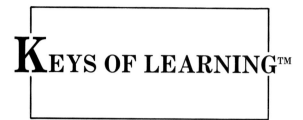

Available from:

Child Guidance®
CBS Toys, A Division of CBS Inc.
41 Madison Avenue
New York, New York 10010

Available at many major toy stores

Description:

Six blocks of different shapes and colors can be fitted into the corresponding holes. Color-coded keys release the blocks. The six blocks can be put together on the top of the toy to form a jigsaw puzzle.

Developmental value:

- Matching and fitting the blocks into the correct holes develops space and form perception.
- Matching the keys to their appropriate blocks enhances color perception.
- Inserting the keys into the key holes improves eye-hand coordination.
- Fitting together the jigsaw puzzle develops space and form perception.

Photo courtesy of
Schwartz Public Relations
Associates, Inc. for
Child Guidance®/CBS Toys

LARGE PARQUETRY BLOCKS AND DESIGNS

Available from:

DLM Teaching Resources
One DLM Park
Allen, Texas 75002

Available through the DLM Teaching Resources catalog

Description:

Wood blocks in six colors and three shapes (square, diamond, and triangle), along with design cards.

Developmental value:

- Copying a design improves space and form perception.

Photo courtesy of
DLM Teaching Resources

LEARNING BY DOING LOTTO GAMES: COLOR

Available from:

Ideal School Supply Company
11000 South Lavergne Avenue
Oak Lawn, Illinois 60453

Available through the Ideal catalog

Description:

Players try to identify and match their lotto cards on the game board.

Developmental value:

- Matching the lotto cards with the game board develops visual perception of color.

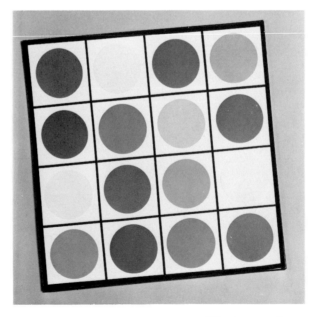

Photo courtesy of
Ideal School Supply Co.

LEARNING BY DOING LOTTO GAMES: SHAPES

Available from:

Ideal School Supply Company
11000 South Lavergne Avenue
Oak Lawn, Illinois 60453

Available through the Ideal catalog

Description:

Players try to identify and match the lotto cards on the game board.

Developmental value:

- Matching the lotto cards with the game board develops visual perception of form.

Photo courtesy of
Ideal School Supply Co.

LIGHTS ALIVE™

Available from:

Tomy Corporation
901 East 233 Street
P.O. Box 6252
Carson, California 90749

Available at many major toy stores

Description:

A self-contained draw-with-light toy. Designs are created by using six different tools across the screen to light up the holes in a specific pattern.

Developmental value:

- Planning and executing designs enhances visual space and form perception.
- Holding and using the various tools helps to refine the dynamic tripod prehension needed for holding a writing instrument.
- Using the tool across the screen to bring light to the design requires motor planning and eye-hand coordination.

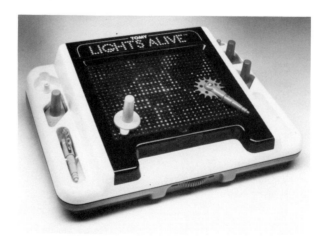

Photo courtesy of
Tomy Corp.

My Little Pony™ MERRY-GO-ROUND GAME

Available from:

Milton Bradley Company
443 Shaker Road
East Longmeadow, Massachusetts 01028-5247

Available at many major toy stores

Description:

Two to four players twirl the merry-go-round and see if the color displayed matches the color of the card in their hands. Matching colors enables the player to stamp his or her score sheet with the corresponding stamp. The first player to fill up all the circles on his or her score sheet is the winner.

Developmental value:

- Matching colors improves color perception skills.
- Picking up and holding the stamps develops pincer grasp ability.
- Stamping within the circles on the score sheet enhances eye-hand coordination.

©1985 Hasbro Bradley, Inc.
All rights reserved.

Photo courtesy of
Milton Bradley Co.

My MAIL BOX

Available from:

Ideal School Supply Company
11000 South Lavergne Avenue
Oak Lawn, Illinois 60453

Available through the Ideal catalog

Description:

A wooden shape sorter with six blocks.

Developmental value:

- Placing the blocks in the correct holes develops form perception.
- Dropping the blocks into the holes improves eye-hand coordination.

Photo courtesy of
Ideal School Supply Co.

PEGBOARD, LARGE PEGBOARD, PEGS, AND PEGBOARD DESIGNS

Available from:

DLM Teaching Resources
One DLM Park
Allen, Texas 75002

Available through the DLM Teaching Resources catalog

Description:

Pegboards and pegs, along with pegboard design cards.

Developmental value:

- Copying a pegboard design pattern improves visual space and form perception.
- Picking up the pegs provides an opportunity to practice pincer grasp and release.
- Placing pegs into the holes improves eye-hand coordination.
- Placing pegs in the large pegboard can improve the ability to reach and cross the midline.

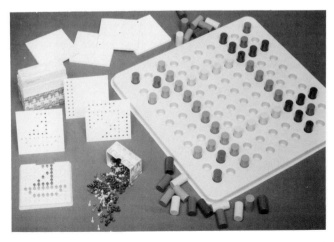

Photo courtesy of
DLM Teaching Resources

PERFECTION®

Available from:

Lakeside
495 Post Road East
Westport, Connecticut 06880

Available at many major toy stores

Description:

Players rush to properly position 25 geometric forms in the playing base before sixty seconds elapse and the playing pieces pop out of position.

Developmental value:

- Matching the playing pieces to their holes improves space and form perception.
- Picking up and letting go of each playing piece develops pincer grasp and release.

Photo courtesy of
Gerald Freeman, Inc.
Public Relations for
Lakeside

PYRAMID PUZZLES

Available from:

Ideal School Supply Company
11000 South Lavergne Avenue
Oak Lawn, Illinois 60453

Available through the Ideal catalog

Description:

Foam rubber puzzle pieces which can be placed on a design card to form patterns.

Developmental value:

- Placing the puzzle pieces onto the pattern can improve visual perception in the area of space, form, color, and size.

Photo courtesy of
Ideal School Supply Co.

RUBBER PARQUETRY

Available from:

Lauri, Inc.
Phillips-Avon, Maine 04966
Available through many special education catalogs

Description:

Crepe foam rubber pieces in a variety of colors and geometric shapes which can be arranged creatively or according to design patterns.

Developmental value:

- Selecting and matching shapes develops form perception.
- Arranging the shapes in patterns improves space perception.

Photo courtesy of
Lauri, Inc.

SEQUENTIAL SORTING BOX

Available from:

Ideal School Supply Company
11000 South Lavergne Avenue
Oak Lawn, Illinois 60453

Available through the Ideal catalog

Description:

Five red wooden blocks are dropped through the geometric shape openings. This is a unique shape sorter in that it can be graded in difficulty through the use of five sliding panels with one to five shape openings.

Developmental value:

- Finding the appropriate block to drop into the corresponding opening develops form perception.
- Fitting the blocks through the holes improves eye-hand coordination.

Photo courtesy of
Ideal School Supply Co.

 SHAPE DISKS

Available from:

Lauri, Inc.
Phillips-Avon, Maine 04966

Available through many special education catalogs

Description:

Crepe foam rubber disks with a single fit-in square, diamond, triangle, or circle.

Developmental value:

- Matching the geometric shapes to the appropriate hole in the disks develops form perception.
- Matching the colors of the shapes and the disks improves color perception.

Photo courtesy of
Lauri, Inc.

#

Available from:

Child Guidance®
CBS Toys, A Division of CBS Inc.
41 Madison Avenue
New York, New York 10010

Available at many major toy stores

Description:

Seven different shapes are sorted and dropped through the corresponding openings.

Developmental value:

- Matching the shapes with their openings develops visual form perception.
- Inserting the shapes into the turtle improves grasping ability and eye-hand coordination.

Photo courtesy of
Schwartz Public Relations
Associates, Inc. for
Child Guidance®/CBS Toys

Sorting and Order Kit

Available from:

Ideal School Supply Company
11000 South Lavergne Avenue
Oak Lawn, Illinois 60453

Available through the Ideal catalog

Description:

Two trays, each with eight compartments for holding a variety of objects. Objects of different shapes and colors are sorted into the compartments.

Developmental value:

- Sorting the shapes promotes form and color perception.
- Picking up each shape develops pincer grasp.

Photo courtesy of
Ideal School Supply Co.

 STRING A LONG™

Available from:

Craft House Corporation
2101 Auburn Avenue
Toledo, Ohio 43696

Available at many major toy stores

Description:

A unique toy which uses string to draw pictures. By putting the pencil on the grid and pressing down gently, all sorts of pictures can be drawn and then "erased" by re-winding the pencil. Plastic stick-ons are included for added decoration.

Developmental value:

- Planning and executing a design develops visual space and form perception.
- Holding the pencil promotes the ability to grasp a writing instrument.
- Rewinding the pencil requires pincer grasp.

Photo courtesy of
Craft House Corp.

SUPERFECTION®

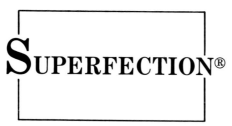

Available from:

Lakeside
495 Post Road East
Westport, Connecticut 06880
Available at many major toy stores

Description:

Players rush to properly assemble thirty-two geometric forms and place them in the base before the two-minute timer runs out and the pieces pop up.

Developmental value:

- Assembling the pieces together improves space and form perception.

Photo courtesy of
Gerald Freeman, Inc.
Public Relations for
Lakeside

TANGRAM AND PUZZLE CARDS

Available from:

DLM Teaching Resources
One DLM Park
Allen, Texas 75002

Available through the DLM Teaching Resources catalog

Description:

A seven-piece black tangram and puzzle design cards. Puzzles can be solved by placing the geometric pieces directly on one of the cards.

Developmental value:

- Solving a tangram puzzle improves space and form perception.

Photo courtesy of
DLM Teaching Resources

TEDDY BEAR SHAPE SORTER

Available from:

Playskool®, Inc.
A Hasbro Bradley Company
1027 Newport Avenue
Pawtucket, Rhode Island 02862

Available at many major toy stores

Description:

A sorting toy with six different shapes.

Developmental value:

- Fitting the blocks into the matching holes develops form perception.

Photo courtesy of
Playskool®, Inc.

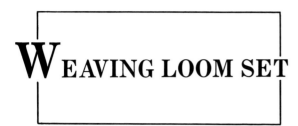

WEAVING LOOM SET

Available from:

Avalon Industries, Inc.
95 Lorimer Street
Brooklyn, New York 11206

Available at many major toy stores

Description:

A loom and loopers to weave into pot holders.

Developmental value:

- Weaving the loopers under and over other loopers develops directionality concepts and visual figure-ground perception.
- Using the fingers to weave the loopers promotes general fine-motor dexterity.

Photo courtesy of
Avalon Industries

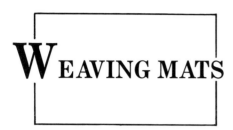

WEAVING MATS

Available from:

Ideal School Supply Company
11000 South Lavergne Avenue
Oak Lawn, Illinois 60453

Available through the Ideal catalog

Description:

Plastic weaving strips which can be woven onto a weaving mat.

Developmental value:

- Weaving the strips under and over the mat improves space and figure-ground perception.
- Manipulating the plastic strips can improve general fine-motor dexterity and eye-hand coordination.

Photo courtesy of
Ideal School Supply Co.

WINDOW PICTURES

Available from:

Binney and Smith
1100 Church Lane
P.O. Box 431
Easton, Pennsylvania 18042

Available at many major toy stores

Description:

Pictures are created by mixing colorful see-through, stick-on shapes.

Developmental value:

- Creating pictures with the stick-on shapes develops visual space and form perception.

Photo courtesy of
Binney and Smith

WUZZLES™ SUPER DELUXE COLORFORMS® PLAY SET

Available from:

Colorforms®
Ramsey, New Jersey 07446

Available at many major toy stores

Description:

Colorforms® pieces are placed onto the picture play board.

Developmental value:

- Placing the Colorforms® figures onto the picture in the appropriate positions (i.e. under the roof, on top of the swing) develops perception of spatial relationships.

©1984 Hasbro Bradley, Inc.
Walt Disney Productions
All Rights Reserved.

Photo courtesy of
Colorforms®

COMPREHENSIVE LISTING OF TOYS BY CATEGORY OF SKILL DEVELOPMENT

FINE-MOTOR DEVELOPMENT

Arm Strength

- "Boom Boom" Stand Up Punching Bag (G. Pierce Toy Co.)
- Bron™ (Lewis Galoob)
- Early Years Ladder (Achievement Products®)
- Forward Pass (DLM Teaching Resources)
- Snap-Lock® Beads (Fisher-Price)

Dynamic Tripod Writing Grasp

- Dapper Dan™ (Smethport Specialty)
- Doodle Balls (Smethport Specialty)
- Light and Learn™ (Milton Bradley)
- Lights Alive™ (Tomy Corp.)
- Magna-Doodle® Magnetic Drawing Toy (Ideal®)
- Rub N' Play™ Transfers (Colorforms®)
- String A Long (Craft House Corporation)
- Tickle Bee® (Schaper)
- Wuzzles® Color N' Play™ (Colorforms®)

Elbow Extension (see also Reach)

- Foam Hockey Set (Achievement Products®)
- Frisbee® Disc (Wham-0®)
- Indoor/Outdoor Shuffleboard (Achievement Products®)

Extended Index Finger

- Ants in the Pants® (Schaper)
- Aqua Action™ Games (Tomy)

- Big Mouth Singers® (Child Guidance®)
- Electronic Musical Phone™ (Playskool®)
- Hungry Hungry Hippos® (Milton Bradley)
- Mr. Mouth® (Tomy)
- Push 'N Pop® Phone (Tomy)
- Rebound® Game (Ideal®)
- Skill Squares™ (Tomy)
- Snappy Shots® (Tomy)
- Stellar™ and Robotman™ Stuffed Figures (Kenner®)
- Tic-Tac-Toad® (Synergistics Research)
- Travel Shut the Box™ (Milton Bradley)
- Wee Wonderful Waterfuls® (Tomy)

Forearm Pronation

- Curious Critters™ (Tomy)
- Twist 'N' Turn (Achievement Products®)

Forearm Supination

- Curious Critters™ (Tomy)
- Kitty in the Kegs™ (Child Guidance®)
- Magic "8 Ball"® (Ideal®)
- Nuts 'N Bolts™ (Child Guidance®)
- Twist 'N' Turn (Achievement Products®)

General Fine-Motor Dexterity

- Barrel of Monkeys® (Lakeside)
- Bed Bugs™ (Milton Bradley)
- Cootie® (Schaper)
- Crayola® Yarn Pictures (Binney and Smith)
- Giggle Gang™ (Lakeside)
- Little Driver's Dashboard® (Tomy)
- Mop Top Hair Shop™ Playset (Kenner®)
- Numbers Up® (Milton Bradley)
- Robo Strux™ (Tomy)
- Sesame Street® Busy Poppin' Pals® (Child Guidance®)
- Shuffletown School™ Playset (Hasbro Bradley)
- Weaving Loom Set (Avalon)
- Weaving Mats (Ideal School Supply)
- Wuzzles™ Color N' Play™ (Colorforms®)

Grasp/Release

- Form Fitter™ (Child Guidance®)
- Shapey Turtle® (Child Guidance®)
- Stuff It!™ (Lakeside)
- Texture Board (Achievement Products®)

Hand Strength

- Air-Mazing Games™ (Tomy)
- Bron™ (Lewis Galoob)
- Cobbler's Bench (Playskool®)
- Doggone Dog® (Tomy)
- Doodle Balls (Smethport)
- Electronic Musical Phone™ (Playskool®)
- Giggle Gang™ (Lakeside)
- Incredible Thrasher™ (Lewis Galoob)
- Kaboomers® Indoor/Outdoor Paddle Game (Ideal®)
- Large Pegboard and Pegs Set (Lauri)
- Locktagons (Lauri)
- Magnastiks™ (Childcraft®)
- Mop Top Hair Shop™ Playset (Kenner®)
- Plasticine® Barrel of Fun™ (Colorforms®)
- Puff-Push (Achievement Products®)
- Rub-A-Dub® Doggie Bathland™ (Child Guidance®)
- Silly Putty (Binney and Smith)

Isolated Finger Function

- Big Mouth Singers® (Child Guidance®)
- Little Tooter Trumpet® (Tomy)
- Mickey Mouse Talking Phone (Hasbro Bradley)
- Popoids™ Cosmic Concert™ (Tomy)
- Push 'N Pop® Phone (Tomy)
- Sesame Street® Finger Puppets (Child Guidance®)
- Stay Alive® (Milton Bradley)
- Talking Mickey Mouse (Child Guidance®)
- Tiny Fingers™ (Tomy)
- Tomy® Tutor Play Computer™ (Tomy)
- Tutor Typer® (Tomy)

Lateral Pinch

- Break Dancer™ (Tomy)

Pincer Grasp/Release

- Battleship® (Milton Bradley)
- Beads 'N Baubles (Lauri)
- Bed Bugs™ (Milton Bradley)
- Big Pegboard and Stackable Pegs (Ideal School Supply)
- Build A Better Burger® (Lakeside)
- Chinese Checkers (Steven Mfg.)
- Curious Critters™ (Tomy)
- Deluxe Aggravation® (Lakeside)
- Don't Spill the Beans® (Schaper®)
- Dragon® Chinese Checkers (Milton Bradley)
- Etch A Sketch® (Ohio Art)
- Formset Puzzles (Ideal School Supply)
- Fisher-Price Bubble Mower (Fisher-Prince)
- Ghosts!® (Milton Bradley)
- Hi-Ho! Cherry-O® Game (Western Publishing)
- Hilarious Hats™ (Tomy)
- Hi-Q® Game (Ideal®)
- Hungry Hungry Hippos® (Milton Bradley)
- Jumbo® Tiddledy Winks (Milton Bradley)
- Kerplunk® Game (Ideal®)
- Lace-A-Puppet (Lauri)
- Lacing Shapes (Lauri)
- Large Abacus (DLM Teaching Resources)
- Large Colored Beads and Patterns (Ideal School Supply)
- Large Pegboard and Pegs Set (Lauri)
- Leverage™ (Milton Bradley)
- Lite-Brite® (Hasbro Bradley)
- Magnastiks™ (Childcraft®)
- Magnetic Pic-Up Stix (Steven Mfg.)
- Mickey Mouse Talking Phone (Hasbro Bradley)
- Mighty Motor Boats® (Tomy)
- My Little Pony™ Merry-Go-Round Game (Milton Bradley)
- Numbers Up® (Milton Bradley)
- Oh Chute! (Schaper®)
- Operation® (Milton Bradley)
- Past Planes® Collection (Tomy)
- Paul Bunyan Giant Wooden Stix (Steven Mfg.)
- Pegboard, Large Pegboard, Pegs, and Pegboard Designs (DLM Teaching Resources)

- Perfection® (Lakeside)
- Pocket Pets® (Tomy)
- Rebound® Game (Ideal®)
- Robo Strux™ (Tomy)
- Score Four® (Lakeside)
- Scurry Furries® (Tomy)
- Sewing Cards (Colorforms®)
- Sorting and Order Kit (Ideal School Supply)
- Stamp-A-Shape (Lauri)
- Stay Alive® (Milton Bradley)
- String A Long (Craft House Corp.)
- Table Toppers® Stunt Pilot (Tomy)
- Travel Shut the Box™ (Milton Bradley)
- Tomy® Tubbies™ (Tomy)
- Twelve Teepees Memory® (Milton Bradley)

Reach

- Creative Railway (Little Tikes®)
- Pegboard, Large Pegboard, Pegs, and Pegboard Designs (DLM Teaching Resources)
- Shuffletown School™ Playset (Hasbro Bradley)

Scissors Use

- Mop Top Hair Shop™ Playset (Kenner®)

Wrist Extension

- Air Jammer® Bug Scrammer (Tomy)
- Bron™ (Lewis Galoob)
- Doggone Dog® (Tomy)
- Drive 'N Play™ Console (Child Guidance®)
- Frisbee® Disc (Wham-O®)
- Go Go Guys™ (Tomy)
- Reck 'N Roll Car™ (Tomy)
- Ring Toss (Lauri)

Wrist Rotation

- Frisbee® Disc (Wham-O®)
- Mop Top Hair Shop™ Playset (Kenner®)

SENSORY DEVELOPMENT

Auditory Discrimination; Sound Sequencing; Auditory Memory

- Big Mouth Singers® (Child Guidance®)
- Electronic Musical Phone™ (Playskool®)
- Simon® (Milton Bradley)

Kinesthetic Input

- Plasticine® Barrel of Fun™ (Colorforms®)
- Long Squishy Walking Mat (Achievement Products®)
- Redskin® Finger Paint (Milton Bradley)
- Stencil Set (Avalon)

Proprioceptive Input

- Beginner's Individual Jumper (Achievement Products®)
- Big Bounce (G. Pierce Toy Co.)
- Super Jump Pogo Stick (G. Pierce Toy Co.)

Tactile Discrimination

- Feel and Match - Textures (Lauri)
- Multi-Sensory Cubes and Spheres (Ideal School Supply)
- Texture Board (Achievement Products®)
- Touch and Tell (Ideal School Supply)

Tactile Stimulation

- Mop Top Hair Shop™ Playset (Kenner®)
- Multi-Texture Puzzles (Lauri)
- Plasticine® Barrel of Fun™ (Colorforms®)
- Redskin® Finger Paint (Milton Bradley)
- Rub-A-Dub® Doggie Bathland™ (Child Guidance®)
- Sand and Water Table (Ideal School Supply)
- Scurry Furries® (Tomy)
- Tomy® Tubbies™ (Tomy)
- Touch and Tell (Ideal School Supply)
- Tubtown® Merry-Go-Round (Lakeside)
- Tubtown Sea Circus® (Lakeside)

Vestibular Stimulation

- Teeter-For-Two (Little Tikes®)

Visual Attention
- Clown Kaleidoscope (Steven Mfg.)

Visual Memory
- Build A Better Burger® (Lakeside)

Visual Sequencing
- Large Colored Beads and Patterns (Ideal School Supply)

Visual Tracking
- Air-Mazing Games™ (Tomy)
- Hungry Hungry Hippos® (Milton Bradley)
- Large Colored Beads and Patterns (Ideal School Supply)
- Roll-A-Ball (Achievement Products®)
- Sewing Cards (Colorforms®)
- Skill Squares™ (Tomy)
- Tracking Association Cards (DLM Teaching Resources)
- Visual Tracking Cards (Ideal School Supply)
- Wee Wonderful Waterfuls® (Tomy)

SENSORY-MOTOR DEVELOPMENT

Balance and Equilibrium Reactions
- Balance Disk (Ideal School Supply)
- Beginner's Individual Jumper (Achievement Products®)
- Big Bounce (G. Pierce Toy Co.)
- Clip-Clop® The Wonder Horse® (Wonder®),
- Deluxe Rocker Balance Square (Achievement Products®)
- Harmon Walking Rail (Ideal School Supply)
- Long Squishy Walking Mat (Achievement Products®)
- One-Legged Balance Stool (Achievement Products®)
- Peppermint Hula Hoop® (Wham-O®)
- Romper Stompers® (Playskool®)
- Sno-Jet (Coleco)
- Spring Bridges (Achievement Products®)
- Super Jump Pogo Stick (G. Pierce Toy Co.)
- Teeter-for-Two (Little Tikes®)
- Twister® (Milton Bradley)

Bilateral Coordination-Upper Extremities

- Beads 'N Baubles (Lauri)
- "Boom Boom" Stand Up Punching Bag (G. Pierce Toy Co.)
- Childcraft® Space Wheels (Childcraft®)
- Clown Kaleidoscope (Steven Mfg.)
- Drive 'N Play™ Console (Child Guidance®)
- Early Years Ladder (Achievement Products®)
- Etch A Sketch® (Ohio Art)
- Erector® Construction System (Ideal®)
- Fisher-Price Bubble Mower (Fisher-Price)
- Foam Hockey Set (Achievement Products®)
- Forward Pass (DLM Teaching Resources)
- Kitty in the Kegs™ (Child Guidance®)
- Large Colored Beads and Patterns (Ideal School Supply)
- Little Driver's Dashboard® (Tomy)
- Locktagons (Lauri)
- NHL Stanley Cup Play-Off Hockey (Coleco)
- Nuts 'N Bolts™ (Child Guidance®)
- Official "Boom Boom" Bop Bag (G. Pierce Toy Co.)
- One Dozen Counting Eggs (Child Guidance®)
- Peg-A-Car (Lauri)
- Popoids™ Cosmic Concert™ (Tomy)
- Popoids™ Cosmic Crackbot™ Set (Tomy)
- Rainbow Chain™ (Child Guidance®)
- Sesame Street® Traveling Band™ (Child Guidance®)
- Silly Putty (Binney and Smith)
- Snap-Lock® Beads (Fisher-Price)
- Snappy Shots® (Tomy)
- Stack 'N' Tumble Clowns™ (Lakeside)
- Stringing Wood Beads (Playskool®)
- Stuff Yer Face™ (Milton Bradley)
- Table Toppers™ Stunt Pilot (Tomy)
- Teeter-for-Two (Little Tikes®)
- Tinkertoy® Building Sets (Child Guidance®)
- Turnin' Turbo Dashboard™ (Tomy)
- Twist 'N' Turn (Achievement Products®)
- Walt Disney© Mini Golf (HG Industries)

Bilateral Coordination-Lower Extremities

- Beginner's Individual Jumper (Achievement Products®)
- Big Bounce (G. Pierce Toy Co.)
- Early Years Ladder (Achievement Products®)

- Jump Board (Ideal School Supply)
- Little Trike (Little Tikes®)
- Super Jump Pogo Stick (G. Pierce Toy Co.)
- Wooden Foot Placement Ladder (Achievement Products®)

Body Awareness

- Be Ba Bo Image Unit (Ideal School Supply)
- Beginner's Individual Jumper (Achievement Products®)
- Body Parts Puzzle (Lauri)
- Early Years Ladder (Achievement Products®)
- Geo Dome (Achievement Products®)
- Giggle Gang™ (Lakeside)
- Mr. Potato Head® Family (Hasbro Bradley)
- Peppermint Hula Hoop® (Wham-O®)
- Plastic Hoops and Hoop Holders (Achievement Products®)
- Spring Bridges (Achievement Products®)
- Teeter-for-Two (Little Tikes®)
- Tunnel of Fun (G. Pierce Toy Co.)
- Twister® (Milton Bradley)

Eye-Foot Coordination

- Get In Shape, Girl!™ Rhythm and Ribbons™ (Hasbro Bradley)
- Hackey Sack® Footbag (Wham-O®)
- Romper Stompers® (Playskool®)
- Wooden Foot Placement Ladder (Achievement Products®)

Eye-Hand Coordination

- Air-Mazing Games™ (Tomy)
- Ants in the Pants® (Schaper®)
- Aqua Action™ Games (Tomy)
- Barrel of Monkeys® (Lakeside)
- Battleship® (Milton Bradley)
- Beads 'N Baubles (Lauri)
- Beano Bean Bag Set (Ideal School Supply)
- Bed Bugs™ (Milton Bradley)
- Big Bird Xylophone (Child Guidance®)
- Big Mouth Singers® (Child Guidance®)
- Big Pegboard and Stackable Pegs (Ideal School Supply)
- Break Dancer® (Tomy)
- Build A Better Burger® (Lakeside)
- Burger King* Whopper* Sandwich Stacking Game (Tomy)
- Childcraft® Space Wheels (Childcraft®)

- Chinese Checkers (Steven Mfg.)
- Cobbler's Bench (Playskool®)
- Colored Inch Cubes, Designs, and Designs in Perspective (DLM Teaching Resources)
- Cootie® (Schaper®)
- Crayola® Little Design Machine (Binney and Smith)
- Crayola® Yarn Pictures (Binney and Smith)
- Creative Railway (Little Tikes®)
- Dapper Dan™ (Smethport Specialty)
- Deluxe Aggravation® (Lakeside)
- Don't Break the Ice® (Schaper®)
- Don't Spill the Beans® (Schaper®)
- Doodle Balls (Smethport Specialty)
- Dragon® Chinese Checkers (Milton Bradley)
- Electronic Musical Phone™ (Playskool®)
- Erector® Construction System (Ideal®)
- Foam Hockey Set (Achievement Products®)
- Form Fitter™ (Child Guidance®)
- Forward Pass (DLM Teaching Resources)
- Frisbee® Disc (Wham-O®)
- Garfield© Giant Ball Darts (Synergistics Research)
- Happy Sound™ Tools (Tomy)
- Hi-Q® Game (Ideal®)
- Hungry Hungry Hippos® (Milton Bradley)
- Indoor/Outdoor Shuffleboard (Achievement Products®)
- Jumbo® Tiddledy Winks (Milton Bradley)
- Kaboomers® Indoor/Outdoor Paddle Game (Ideal®)
- Keys of Learning™ (Child Guidance®)
- Lace-A-Puppet (Lauri)
- Lacing Shapes (Lauri)
- Lacing Soldier (Achievement Products®)
- Large Pegboard and Pegs Set (Lauri)
- Learning Tower™ (Child Guidance®)
- Leverage™ (Milton Bradley)
- Light and Learn™ (Milton Bradley)
- Lights Alive™ (Tomy)
- Lite-Brite® (Hasbro Bradley)
- Locktagons (Lauri)
- Lollipop Paddles Set (Achievement Products®)
- Magnetic Pic-Up Stix (Steven Mfg.)
- Mr. Mouth® (Tomy)
- Mr. Potato Head® Family (Hasbro Bradley)
- My Little Pony® Merry-Go-Round Game (Milton Bradley)

- My Mail Box (Ideal School Supply)
- NHL Stanley Cup Play-Off Hockey (Coleco)
- Numbers Up (Milton Bradley)
- Oh Chute! (Schaper®)
- Operation® (Milton Bradley)
- Pac-Man™ Magnetic Maze (Tomy)
- Paul Bunyan Giant Wooden Stix (Steven Mfg.)
- Peg-A-Car (Lauri)
- Pegboard, Large Pegboard, Pegs, and Pegboard Designs (DLM Teaching Resources)
- Popoids™ Cosmic Concert (Tomy)
- Popoids™ Cosmic Crackbot™ Set (Tomy)
- Power Jet™ Hockey (Coleco)
- Rainbow Chain™ (Child Guidance®)
- Rainbow Stacker™ (Lakeside)
- Rebound® Game (Ideal®)
- Ring Toss (Lauri)
- Rub-A-Dub® Doggie Bathland™ (Child Guidance®)
- Score Four® (Lakeside)
- Sequential Sorting Box (Ideal School Supply)
- Sewing Cards (Colorforms®)
- Shapey Turtle® (Child Guidance®)
- Shuffletown School™ Playset (Hasbro Bradley)
- Skill Squares™ (Tomy)
- Snork™ Ball (Tomy)
- Spin Around Clowns™ (Lakeside)
- Stack 'N' Tumble Clowns™ (Lakeside)
- Stacrobats (Lauri)
- Stencil Set (Avalon)
- Stringing Wood Beads (Playskool®)
- Stuff It!™ (Lakeside)
- Stuff Yer Face™ (Milton Bradley)
- Table Topper™ Stunt Pilot (Tomy)
- Take-Apart Workbench (Playskool®)
- Texture Board (Achievement Products®)
- Tickle-Bee® (Schaper®)
- Tic-Tac-Toad® (Synergistic Research)
- Tinkertoy® Building Sets (Child Guidance®)
- Tomy® Tutor Play Computer (Tomy)
- Tracking Association Cards (DLM Teaching Resources)
- Tubtown® Merry-Go-Round (Lakeside)
- Tubtown Sea Circus® (Lakeside)
- Tutor Typer® (Tomy)

- Twist 'N' Turn (Achievement Products®)
- Walt Disney© Mini Golf (HG Industries)
- Weaving Mats (Ideal School Supply)
- Wuzzles™ Bean Bag Game (Synergistics Research)
- Wuzzles™ Color N' Play® (Colorforms®)

Gross-Motor Coordination

- Geo-Dome (Achievement Products®)
- Get In Shape, Girl!™ Rhythm and Ribbons™ (Hasbro Bradley)
- Teeter-for-Two (Little Tikes®)

Midline Crossing

- Creative Railway (Little Tikes®)
- Get In Shape, Girl!™ Rhythm and Ribbons™ (Hasbro Bradley)
- Large Abacus (DLM Teaching Resources)
- Pegboard, Large Pegboard, Pegs, and Pegboard Designs (DLM Teaching Resources)
- Power Jet™ Hockey (Coleco)
- Twister® (Milton Bradley)

Motor Planning

- Childcraft® Space Wheels (Childcraft®)
- Creative Railway (Little Tikes®)
- Drive 'N Play™ Console (Child Guidance®)
- Early Years Ladder (Achievement Products®)
- Erector® Construction System (Ideal®)
- Etch A Sketch® (Ohio Art)
- Geo-Dome (Achievement Products)
- Happy Sound™ Tools (Tomy)
- Lacing Soldier (Achievement Products®)
- Lights Alive® (Tomy)
- Mop Top Hair Shop™ Playset (Kenner®)
- Operation® (Milton Bradley)
- Pac-Man™ Magnetic Maze (Tomy)
- Peppermint Hula Hoop® (Wham-O®)
- Plastic Hoops and Hoop Holders (Achievement Products®)
- Plasticine® Barrel of Fun™ (Colorforms®)
- Spring Bridges (Achievement Products®)
- Take-Apart Workbench (Playskool®)
- Teeter-for-Two (Little Tikes®)
- Tunnel of Fun (G. Pierce Toy Co.)
- Twister® (Milton Bradley)
- Wooden Foot Placement Ladder (Achievement Products®)

Right-Left Discrimination

- Be Ba Bo Image Unit (Ideal School Supply)
- Twister® (Milton Bradley)

VISUAL-PERCEPTUAL DEVELOPMENT

Color Perception

- Attribute Blocks (Ideal School Supply)
- Bed Bugs™ (Milton Bradley)
- Big Bird Xylophone (Child Guidance®)
- Big Mouth Singers® (Child Guidance®)
- Electronic Musical Phone™ (Playskool®)
- Fit-A-Space (Lauri)
- Happy Sound™ Tools (Tomy)
- Keys of Learning™ (Child Guidance®)
- Kitty in the Kegs™ (Child Guidance®)
- Learning by Doing Lotto Games: Color (Ideal School Supply)
- Learning Tower™ (Child Guidance®)
- Multi-Sensory Cubes and Spheres (Ideal School Supply)
- My Little Pony™ Merry-Go-Round Game (Milton Bradley)
- Nuts 'N Bolts™ (Child Guidance®)
- Pyramid Puzzles (Ideal School Supply)
- Shape Disks (Lauri)
- Sorting and Order Kit (Ideal School Supply)
- Stacrobats (Lauri)
- Texture Board (Achievement Products®)
- Twister® (Milton Bradley)

Depth Perception

- Forward Pass (DLM Teaching Resources)
- Wooden Foot Placement Ladder (Achievement Products®)

Directionality Perception

- Pac-Man™ Magnetic Maze™ (Tomy)
- Score Four® (Lakeside)
- Weaving Loom Set (Avalon)

Figure-Ground Perception

- Bed Bugs™ (Milton Bradley)
- Hidden Objects (Idea School Supply)

- Magnetic Pic-Up Stix (Steven Mfg.)
- Paul Bunyan Giant Wooden Stix (Steven Mfg.)
- Score Four® (Lakeside)
- Tracking Association Cards (DLM Teaching Resources)
- Weaving Loom Set (Avalon)

Form Perception

- Attribute Blocks (Ideal School Supply)
- Build A Better Burger® (Lakeside)
- Cookie Monster Shape Muncher® (Playskool®)
- Crayola® Little Design Machine (Binney and Smith)
- Design Blocks and Patterns (Ideal School Supply)
- Doodle Balls (Smethport Specialty)
- Etch A Sketch® (Ohio Art)
- Fit-A-Space (Lauri)
- Fit-In Perception Puzzles (Lauri)
- Form Fitter™ (Child Guidance®)
- Keys of Learning™ (Child Guidance®)
- Large Parquetry Blocks and Designs (DLM Teaching Resources)
- Learning By Doing Lotto Games: Shapes (Ideal School Supply)
- Lights Alive™ (Tomy)
- Magna-Doodle® Magnetic Drawing Toy (Ideal®)
- Magnastiks™ (Childcraft®)
- Multi-Sensory Cubes and Spheres (Ideal School Supply)
- Multi-Texture Puzzles (Lauri)
- My Mail Box (Ideal School Supply)
- Peg-A-Car (Lauri)
- Pegboard, Large Pegboard, Pegs, and Pegboard Designs (DLM Teaching Resources)
- Perfection® (Lakeside)
- Popoids™ Cosmic Crackbot™ Set (Tomy)
- Pyramid Puzzles (Ideal School Supply)
- Rubber Parquetry (Lauri)
- Sequential Sorting Box (Ideal School Supply)
- Shape Disks (Lauri)
- Shapey Turtle® (Child Guidance®)
- Sorting and Order Kit (Ideal School Supply)
- Stencil Set (Avalon)
- String A Long (Craft House)
- Superfection® (Lakeside)
- Tangram and Puzzle Cards (DLM Teaching Resources)
- Teddy Bear Shape Sorter® (Playskool®)

- Tinkertoy® Building Sets (Child Guidance®)
- Window Pictures (Binney and Smith)

Size Perception

- Attribute Blocks (Ideal School Supply)
- Formset Puzzles (Ideal School Supply)
- Kitty in the Kegs™ (Child Guidance®)
- Learning Tower™ (Child Guidance®)
- Multi-Sensory Cubes and Spheres (Ideal School Supply)
- Nuts 'N Bolts™ (Child Guidance®)
- Pyramid Puzzles (Ideal School Supply)
- Rainbow Stacker™ (Lakeside)

Space Perception

- Attribute Blocks (Ideal School Supply)
- Childcraft® Space Wheels (Childcraft®)
- Colored Inch Cubes, Designs, and Designs in Perspective (DLM Teaching Resources)
- Crayola® Little Design Machine (Binney and Smith)
- Design Blocks and Patterns (Ideal School Supply)
- Don't Break the Ice® (Schaper®)
- Doodle Balls (Smethport Specialty)
- Drive 'N Play™ Console (Child Guidance®)
- Etch A Sketch® (Ohio Art)
- Fit-In Perception Puzzles (Lauri)
- Keys of Learning™ (Child Guidance®)
- Large Parquetry Blocks and Designs (DLM Teaching Resources)
- Large Pegboard and Pegs Set (Lauri)
- Lights Alive™ (Tomy)
- Magna-Doodle® Magnetic Drawing Toy (Ideal®)
- Magnastiks™ (Childcraft®)
- Magnetic Pic-Up Stix (Steven Mfg.)
- Multi-Texture Puzzles (Lauri)
- Pac-Man™ Magnetic Maze™ (Tomy)
- Paul Bunyan Giant Wooden Stix (Steven Mfg.)
- Pegboard, Large Pegboard, Pegs, and Pegboard Designs (DLM Teaching Resources)
- Perfection® (Lakeside)
- Popoids™ Cosmic Crackbot™ Set (Tomy)
- Pyramid Puzzles (Ideal School Supply)
- Rubber Parquetry (Lauri)
- Stamp-A-Shape (Lauri)

- Stencil Set (Avalon)
- String A Long™ (Craft House)
- Superfection® (Lakeside)
- Tangram and Puzzle Cards (DLM Teaching Resources)
- Tinkertoy® Building Sets (Child Guidance®)
- Weaving Mats (Ideal School Supply)
- Window Pictures (Binney and Smith)
- Wuzzles™ Color N' Play (Colorforms®)
- Wuzzles™ Super Deluxe Colorforms® Play Set (Colorforms®)

TOY CATALOGS, DEALERS, AND SUPPLIERS

The Able Child
325 West 11th Street
New York City 10014

Achievement Products® Inc.
P.O. Box 547
Mineola, New York 11501

Childcraft Education Corporation
20 Kilmer Road
Edison, New Jersey 08818

Constructive Playthings
1227 East 119th Street
Grandview, Missouri 64030

Discovery Toys
400 Ellinwood Way
Pleasant Hill, California 94523

DLM Teaching Resources
One DLM Park
Allen, Texas 75002

Educational Teaching Aids
159 West Kinzie Street
Chicago, Illinois 60610

Ideal School Supply Company
11000 South Lavergne Avenue
Oak Lawn, Illinois 60453

INDEX

Jl